VIRTUAL DOONESBURY

VIRTUAL DOONESBURY

Recent Doonesbury Books by G.B. Trudeau

Read My Lips, Make My Day, Eat Quiche and Die!
Give Those Nymphs Some Hooters!
You're Smokin' Now, Mr. Butts!
I'd Go With the Helmet, Ray
Welcome to Club Scud!
What Is It, Tink, Is Pan in Trouble?
Quality Time on Highway 1
Washed Out Bridges and Other Disasters
In Search of Cigarette Holder Man
Doonesbury Nation

In Large Format

The Doonesbury Chronicles
Doonesbury's Greatest Hits
The People's Doonesbury
Doonesbury Dossier: The Reagan Years
Doonesbury Deluxe: Selected Glances Askance
Recycled Doonesbury: Second Thoughts on a Gilded Age
Action Figure!
The Portable Doonesbury
Flashbacks: Twenty-five Years of Doonesbury

A DOONESBURY BOOK

VIRTUAL DOONESBURY

VIRTUAL DOONESBURY

BY G. B. TRUDEAU

Andrews and McMeel
A Universal Press Syndicate Company
Kansas City

DOONESBURY is distributed internationally by Universal Press Syndicate.

ISBN: 0-8362-1032-8

Library of Congress Catalog Card Number: 96-84523

"I'm not running this year, so I can tell the truth."

—Senator Alfonse D'Amato

THANKS FOR THE BEER, ROLAND...
NO PROB, RICK. I'D JOIN YOU, BUT I'VE GOT ANOTHER LIVE O.J. FEED AT 7:45!

NO DISRESPECT INTENDED TO YOU PRINT BOYS, BUT I GOTTA TELL YOU, TELEVISION OWNS THIS STORY, OWNS IT!
©B Trudeau

GUYS LIKE ME TAKE A LOT OF HITS FOR OUR LIMOS AND CATERED MEALS AND WINNEBAGOS, BUT LEMME TELL YOU, WE'RE EARNING 'EM!

I SEE YOU'VE ATTRACTED YOUR OWN HOMELESS.
NO, THAT'S MY CREW.
DON'T GIVE THEM ANYTHING, BY THE WAY.

YEAH, IT'S REDFERN. JUST CHECKING IN...
FZZZ!

WHAT?... NO! NO WAY! I WAS SENT OUT HERE TO COVER THE LEGAL ISSUES!... THAT WAS VERY CLEAR!
FZZZ

NO, C'MON, MAN, THAT'S JUST CHEAP AND DEGRADING... I SHOULDN'T HAVE TO BE... ED? ED? DAMN!
©B Trudeau

BAD NEWS?
YEAH. I HAVE TO COVER YOU.

YOU'VE BEEN ASSIGNED TO COVER ME?
THE PAPER WANTS COVERAGE OF HOW THE NETWORK STARS ARE DOING!

PLUM ASSIGNMENT, HUH? THE TRIAL OF THE CENTURY, AND I GET TO REPORT ON OTHER REPORTERS!
YEAH... YEAH, I CAN SEE HOW THAT COULD BE A LITTLE ROUGH ON YOU, PRIDE-WISE...
©B Trudeau

WHY DON'T I FEED YOU THE QUESTIONS? MIGHT TAKE SOME OF THE PRESSURE OFF.
MAYBE I COULD JOB IT OUT, PAY SOME KID...

WELL, WE MIGHT AS WELL GET THIS OVER WITH...
RICK, I KNOW HOW HARD IT MUST BE TO INTERVIEW A PEER, ESPECIALLY A BIG STAR...

...BUT REMEMBER, THE ONLY DIFFERENCE BETWEEN US IS A HUGE SALARY DIFFERENTIAL. OTHER THAN THAT, I'M JUST A REPORTER, MUCH LIKE YOURSELF.

THANK YOU, ROLAND. I'LL KEEP THAT IN MIND.
GREAT.
GB Trudeau

SO WHAT'S THE DEAL WITH THE DORKY SIDEBURNS?
VIEWERS LIKE 'EM. AT LEAST THE FOCUS GROUP DID.

WHY DO I DO IT? WHAT DRIVES ME TO EXCELLENCE IN BROADCAST JOURNALISM? IS IT THE MONEY? THE GLAMOUR? THE PERKS?

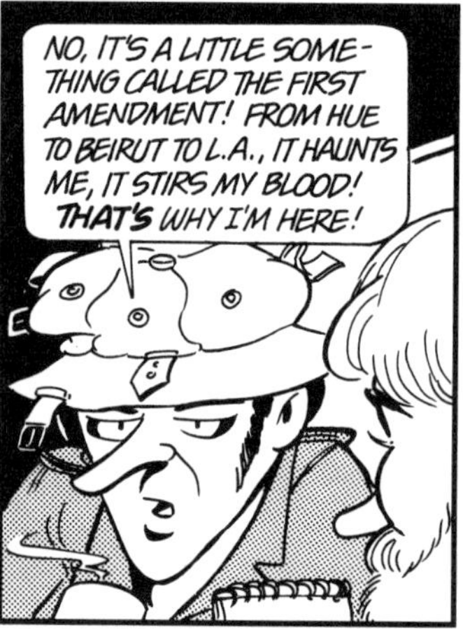
NO, IT'S A LITTLE SOMETHING CALLED THE FIRST AMENDMENT! FROM HUE TO BEIRUT TO L.A., IT HAUNTS ME, IT STIRS MY BLOOD! THAT'S WHY I'M HERE!

SO DID YOU GET ALL THAT?
YEAH, BUT I CAN'T USE IT. IT'S PRETTY BORING...
GB Trudeau

PETER, BEING A JOURNALIST COVERING THE O.J. TRIAL IS A DAUNTING TASK, REQUIRING STAMINA, JUDGMENT AND FINELY HONED COMMUNICATIONS SKILLS...
O.J. PRESS

BUT YOU KNOW, PETER, THOSE WHO COVER THE PRESS ALSO SERVE! CASE IN POINT, WASHINGTON POST MEDIA REPORTER RICK REDFERN, HERE WITH ME NOW...
PRESS

SO WHAT'S IT LIKE COVERING ME, RICK?
WELL, IT'S TOUGH, ROLAND. I'M OUT THERE IN THE FIELD, DAY AFTER DAY, WITH NO SELF-RESPECT AT ALL—NONE!

BUT YOU'RE A PRO. YOU GET THE JOB DONE, RIGHT?
NO, ACTUALLY, I'VE PRETTY MUCH REFUSED TO DO IT.
GB Trudeau

I WISH YOU'D BRING SAM TO SEE ME, B.D.— I MISS HER SO MUCH...

BOOPSIE, SHE'S ONLY THREE. I DON'T THINK A TWO-HOUR DRIVE WITH A BAG OVER HER HEAD IS SUCH A GOOD IDEA!
MAYBE THEY'D MAKE AN EXCEPTION FOR HER...

THIS TRIAL IS SO LONG, I JUST FEEL LIKE SHE'S GROWING UP WITHOUT ME...

ZONKER, WHO'S THIS LADY?
THAT'S YOUR BIRTH MOTHER. ISN'T SHE PRETTY?

THIS IS MOMMY? BUT IT DOESN'T LOOK LIKE MOMMY!
WELL, SHE WAS MUCH YOUNGER, SAMANTHA. THAT'S FROM HER FIRST MOVIE...

WOW... SHE LOOKS SO PRETTY...
DOESN'T SHE?

ZONKER, I THINK MOMMY'S THE MOST BEAUTIFUL LADY IN THE WORLD!
COULD BE...

EXCEPT FOR WHEN SHE CHANNELS FOR UNCLE HUNK-RA.
WELL, HUNK'S GOT A FEW MILES ON HIM, SAM.

ZONKER, WHY ISN'T MOMMY WEARING ANY CLOTHES IN THIS PICTURE?
UM... SHE'S WORKING, SAM...

THAT'S CALLED A PUBLICITY STILL. IT'S FROM "PORKY'S II," A MOVIE YOUR MOMMY WAS IN. SHE PLAYED THIRD GIRL IN SHOWER.

WOW...

WHEN I GROW UP, I WANT TO TAKE SHOWERS, TOO!
WELL, IT'S NOT ALL FUN, SAM. YOU GET WATER IN YOUR EYES.

HI, SWEET-NESS!
MOMMY!

HOW ARE YOU, HONEY? MOMMY MISSES YOU SOMETHING FIERCE!
ME TOO, MAMBO! HOW'S THE TRIAL GO-ING?

CURSED CHILD! YOU DARE TO SPEAK OF THE UNSPEAKABLE? MAY RAVENS PLUCK OUT YOUR IMPUDENT TONGUE!
©B Trudeau

UNCLE HUNK-RA, COULD YOU PUT MOMMY BACK ON, PLEASE?
WHAT'S THAT, SWEET-HEART?

ZONKER, WHEN'S MOMMY COMING HOME?
AS SOON AS JUSTICE IS DONE, SMALL FRY.

HOW LONG WILL THAT TAKE?
NOT SURE. MAYBE SIX MONTHS.

SIX MONTHS? DID YOU SAY SIX MONTHS?
UH-OH... NOW I'VE DONE IT...
©B Trudeau

THAT'S NOTHING! I ONCE HELD MY BREATH FOR TEN YEARS!
WHEW...

SO HOW'S THE KID DOING, ZONKER?
SAM? OH, SHE'S FINE...

FINE? THAT'S A LITTLE HARD TO BELIEVE...
IT IS? WHY?

WELL, C'MON, LOOK AT HER ENVIRONMENT! SHE'S BEING RAISED BY A MEATHEAD, A BIMBO, A 30,000-YEAR-OLD WARRIOR, AND A RECOVERING SURFER!

WHAT'S YOUR POINT, UNCLE DUKE?
I JUST THINK SHE COULD USE A CHANGE OF SCENERY, THAT'S ALL.
©B Trudeau

THIS IS REALLY THE BUDGET, SIR?
JUST A ROUGH DRAFT. WHAT DO YOU THINK?

UH... WELL...
IMPRESSIVE PROFIT MARGIN PER UNIT, NO? "NOTHIN' BUT ORPHANS" COULD BE A REAL MONEY MACHINE!

SIR, I CAN'T HELP NOTICING YOU HAVEN'T BUDGETED A SALARY FOR ME...
©B Trudeau

YOU DON'T SEE ONE FOR ME, EITHER, DO YOU?
NO, BUT I DO SEE A $2 MILLION GOLDEN PARACHUTE.
WHICH I'LL **NEVER** USE! KIDS ARE MY **LIFE** NOW!

THAT BUDGET PRETTY MUCH SAYS IT ALL, HONEY...

IF WE BILL OUT AT $20,000 A POP, "NOTHIN' BUT ORPHANS" COULD CLEAR $350,000 IN THE FIRST **YEAR**!

I DON'T KNOW, SIR. YOU MIGHT BE CHALLENGED ON SOME OF YOUR SUPPOSITIONS ABOUT THE NEEDS OF CHILDREN...
LIKE WHAT?
©B Trudeau

200 CALORIES A DAY?
ADEQUATE. IF WE DON'T LET 'EM TEAR AROUND, **MORE** THAN ADEQUATE!

SIR, WHERE EXACTLY ARE WE GETTING OUR CLIENTS FOR "NOTHIN' BUT ORPHANS"?

THAT'S THE EASY PART, HONEY. WE JUST TAKE 'EM FROM UNDERAGE, UNFIT, UNWED MOTHERS!

OH...
©B Trudeau

BUT ISN'T THAT KIDNAPPING?
NOT FOR MUCH LONGER. IT'S NUMBER THREE IN NEWT'S CONTRACT.

GOOD OL' NEWT! HE CAME THROUGH WITH THE FUNDS FOR OUR FEASIBILITY STUDY!

WE'RE CONDUCTING A FEASIBILITY STUDY, SIR?
YUP. $50,000 WORTH! ONLY PROBLEM IS HE'LL BE EXPECTING ME TO KICK BACK SOME OF IT TO HIS PAC...

YOU'RE THINKING OF SKIPPING RIGHT NOW, AREN'T YOU, SIR?
NO, NO... THIS IS CHICKEN FEED. I'VE GOT TO BE DISCIPLINED.

WHEN ARE YOU GOING TO DO THE FEASIBILITY STUDY, SIR?
I ALREADY HAVE. I STUDIED IT, AND IT'S FEASIBLE.

YOU GOT $50,000 JUST FOR THAT, SIR?
THINK OF IT AS SEED MONEY, HONEY. WE'VE GOT TO UNDERWRITE 35 BEDS!

35? SIR, THAT'S INSANE! HOW CAN WE POSSIBLY CONTROL 35 KIDS?
EASY. DUCT TAPE.

DUCT TAPE?
HONEY, THERE'RE FEW CHILD CARE PROBLEMS THAT CAN'T BE SOLVED WITH DUCT TAPE.

UPS, MA'AM.
OH GOOD, IT'S THE BABY BOTTLES!
Nothin' but Orphans

THAT'S GOING TO BE $247.93, MA'AM. I'LL NEED IT IN CASH...

HOLD ON, PLEASE. I HAVE TO GET THE MONEY FROM OUR COMPTROLLER...

EXCUSE ME, SIR...
YOU HEARD ME—ALL 50 G'S ON THE KNICKS!

EL? LIKE TO GO FOR SOME SOUP?
SHHH! QUIET!

WHY, DUCKS?
I'M SCROLLING THROUGH MY E-MAIL!

DON'T YOU NEED A COMPUTER FOR THAT?
POSSIBLY.
RESEARCHERS STILL AREN'T SURE.

I JUST REMEMBERED! I GET MY E-MAIL AT THE PUBLIC LIBRARY!

YOU DO?
THEY WERE HANDING OUT ADDRESSES TO THE HOMELESS, SO I SNAPPED ONE UP!

WHAT A GREAT IDEA! A PLACE WHERE PROSPECTIVE EMPLOYERS CAN FIND US! DID YOU POST A RESUME?
YUP! NO NIBBLES YET!

THAT'S ODD— WHAT'S YOUR ADDRESS?
LUNATIC @ STREET LEVEL.

SEE, FIRST I CALL UP MY ON-LINE PROVIDER. I JUST TYPE IN "GO: HOMELESS."
TAP! TAP!

THEN I ENTER MY PASSWORD, "ROT:GUT"! BINGO! I'M IN! AND LOOK... I'VE GOT ONE PIECE OF E-MAIL! LET'S OPEN 'ER UP, PRONTO!
TAP! TAP! TAP!

To: All readers.
Seek homeless male with basic computer skills for well-paid, secure job. Free training and mental health care. Contact writer.

ELMONT!
OKAY, THAT'S JUNK MAIL, SO I DELETE IT— LIKE THAT!
TAP! TAP!

Welcome, Elmont! --Helen.
THAT'S HELEN! SHE'S A REGULAR IN THE HOMELESS CHAT GROUP!

Helen, let's meet in Vegas and get married. --Elmont.
ELMONT! YOU CAN'T MARRY HELEN!
TAP! TAP! TAP!

I CAN'T? GOOD LORD! WHY ON EARTH NOT?
WE'VE BEEN OVER THIS A MILLION TIMES. YOU'RE ALREADY MARRIED TO ME!
GBTrudeau

Helen: Bad news. I've been living a lie. --Elmont.
Elmont: Me, too. I'm actually fully clothed.
TAP! TAP! TAP!

ALMOST FINISHED, DUCKS?
COULD BE! NOT SURE! I'M JUST TAKING IT ONE STEP AT A TIME!

EL, THEY'RE ABOUT TO CLOSE...
THEY CAN'T CLOSE! I'M ON OFFICIAL BUSINESS!

WHAT SORT OF OFFICIAL BUSINESS, DUCKS?
WHAT'S IT LOOK LIKE? I'M DOWNLOADING THE LIBRARY OF CONGRESS!

ALL OF IT?
OF COURSE NOT! JUST THE BESTSELLERS.
GBTrudeau

YO, ELMONT...
CAN'T TALK NOW! I'M DOWNLOADING THE LIBRARY OF CONGRESS! A TO Z! SOUP TO NUTS!

WELL, WE GOTTA CLOSE, MAN. WHY DON'T YOU SAVE YOUR WORK AND COME IN AND FINISH UP TOMORROW, OKAY?
GBTrudeau

LET'S SEE WHAT YOU'VE GOT SO FAR... MY, TWELVE BOOKS ON AARDVARKS.
PRINT 'EM OUT! I NEED 'EM TONIGHT!
TAP! TAP!

BIG PROJECT?
YEAH, I GOTTA REPAPER MY CRATE. WINDCHILL PROBLEMS.

MR. SPEAKER, COULD YOU ELABORATE ON YOUR PLAN FOR ABOLISHING HIGH SCHOOL DATING?

LOOK, WHAT I SAID WAS THAT FOUR YEARS OF HIGH SCHOOL FREQUENTLY AMOUNTS TO SUBSIDIZED DATING! GET IT RIGHT FOR A CHANGE!

WHAT I'M QUESTIONING IS WHETHER WE SHOULD BE MAINTAINING A SYSTEM OF EDUCATION JUST SO STUDENTS CAN PURSUE THEIR SOCIAL LIVES!

HOLD IT. DIDN'T HE MARRY HIS GEOMETRY TEACHER?
MUST BE TALKING FROM PAINFUL EXPERIENCE.

MR. SPEAKER? I THINK WE MIGHT WANT TO BACK OFF ON THE CRITICISM OF HIGH SCHOOL AS "SUBSIDIZED DATING"...
WHY? THAT'S EXACTLY WHAT IT IS!

DATING IN HIGH SCHOOLS IS SIMPLY OUT OF CONTROL! IF TAXPAYERS KNEW WHAT WAS GOING ON, THEY'D BE OUTRAGED!

LOOK, I SPEAK FROM BITTER EXPERIENCE! I DATED AND MARRIED ONE OF MY TEACHERS!
THEN ONE DAY I WOKE UP AND SUDDENLY REALIZED SHE WASN'T FIRST LADY MATERIAL!

PERMISSION TO CRINGE, SIR.
I JUST DON'T WANT THAT HAPPENING TO SOME OTHER POOR KID!

THE TRUTH IS, WHEN YOU LOOK AT SOCIETY'S ILLS — TEEN PREGNANCY, UNWED MOTHERS, ABORTION, AIDS — SO MANY OF THEM START WITH HIGH SCHOOL DATING!

THERE ISN'T A HIGH SCHOOL IN THE COUNTRY TODAY WHERE YOU CAN'T JUST WALK UP TO A GIRL AND OPENLY ASK HER FOR A DATE!

IT'S JUST OUT OF CONTROL! IF I WERE RUNNING A HIGH SCHOOL, I'D PUT A STOP TO IT IN A HEARTBEAT!

IF NEWT RAN A HIGH SCHOOL
YOU! I SAW THAT EYE CONTACT!
UM... SHE'S MY SISTER, SIR!

IF NEWT RAN A HIGH SCHOOL.
...AND WE CAN NO LONGER TOLERATE WHAT AMOUNTS TO AFFIRMATIVE ACTION FOR CHRONIC DATERS!

FOUR YEARS OF HIGH SCHOOL IS SIMPLY TOO MUCH TEMPTATION! FOR THAT REASON, I'M OFFICIALLY CANCELING SENIOR YEAR!

ANY QUESTIONS?

UM... HOW DO WE GRADUATE?
YOU DON'T! THAT'S JUST ANOTHER EXCUSE FOR A PARTY!

IF NEWT RAN A HIGH SCHOOL.
I HEREBY DECLARE THIS SCHOOL A DATE-FREE ZONE!

NO LONGER WILL TAXPAYERS BE BURDENED BY A STUDENT POPULATION DISTRACTED FROM THE WORK AT HAND!

YOU'RE FACING ENTRY INTO A TOUGH, DEMANDING ECONOMY! IF YOU'RE NOT READY, YOU'LL BE EATEN ALIVE!

ONLY THROUGH DISCIPLINE AND FOCUS...
WHOA! LOOK AT THE PISTOLS ON THAT NEW FRENCH TEACHER!

IF NEWT RAN A HIGH SCHOOL.
PRINCIPAL GINGRICH? DOES THE NEW ZERO TOLERANCE FOR DATING ALSO APPLY TO THE PROM?

ESPECIALLY THE PROM! DO YOU THINK LOCAL TAXPAYERS SHOULD HAVE TO UNDERWRITE THE SIX-WEEK RUN-UP TO PROM, WHEN NO CLASSWORK GETS DONE?
I MEAN, DO YOU REALLY THINK JOINING THE DECORATION COMMITTEE AND CUTTING OUT LITTLE PAPER EIFFEL TOWERS PREPARES YOU FOR THE REAL WORLD?

NO, BUT IT'S... IT'S FUN.
FUN? SO'S WELFARE! DOES THAT MAKE IT RIGHT?

I DON'T CARE IF IT **IS** THE TRIAL OF THE MILLENNIUM — THIS SEQUESTRATION THING IS **TOTALLY** UNREASONABLE!

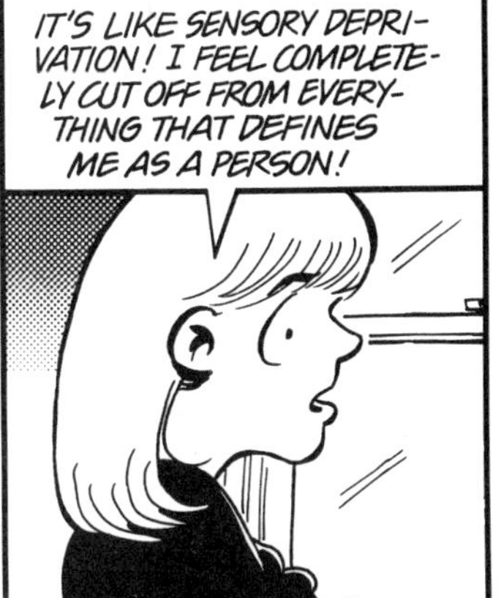
IT'S LIKE SENSORY DEPRIVATION! I FEEL COMPLETELY CUT OFF FROM EVERYTHING THAT DEFINES ME AS A PERSON!

I MEAN, A **WOMAN'S** GOT **URGES!** I'VE GONE WITHOUT FOR THE WHOLE **WINTER!**
©B Trudeau

WHAT'RE YOU TALKING ABOUT? **WE** DID IT LAST MONTH.
NOT THAT, B.D.— SHOPPING! IT'S BEEN 63 **DAYS!**

SHOPPING? THAT'S WHAT YOU MISS THE **MOST?**
YOU'RE NOT A WOMAN, B.D. YOU COULDN'T POSSIBLY UNDERSTAND...

WHY DON'T YOU JUST SHOP BY CATALOG?
I HAVE, BUT IT'S NOT THE SAME. SHOPPING IS VERY TACTILE FOR ME...

THERE'S SOMETHING UNNATURAL ABOUT NOT SHOPPING, SOMETHING UNHOLY. HERE, FEEL MY CREDIT CARDS!
©B Trudeau

WHOA— THEY'RE COLD AS ICE!
AND LOOK—THE MAGNETIC STRIPS ARE FLAKING FROM DISUSE!

ROOM CHECK, MS. BOOPSTEIN!
RAP
RAP

UM...SHE'S IN THE SHOWER, DEPUTY!

TELL HER THE BUS LEAVES FOR THE COURTHOUSE AT 8:30 SHARP!
I SURE WILL! GOOD NIGHT!
©B Trudeau

THAT WAS CLOSE...
HURRY, B.D.! SAKS CLOSES IN AN HOUR!

I CAN'T **BELIEVE** I'M IN A DEPARTMENT STORE, B.D.! I CAN **BREATHE** AGAIN!

POOR O.J. — HE HASN'T BEEN ABLE TO SHOP SINCE LAST SPRING! HOW'S HE SUPPOSED TO LOOK HIS BEST IN COURT?

I WONDER IF I SHOULD GET HIM A NEW TIE...
GET HIM A **TIE?** WHAT, ARE YOU **NUTS?**

YOU THINK THE JUDGE WOULD DIS-APPROVE?
OH, NO, NOT AT ALL! GET HIM SOME NEW GLOVES WHILE YOU'RE AT IT!

B.D., I FEEL LIKE A NEW WOMAN!
THAT'S BE-CAUSE YOU'RE $600 LIGHTER.

WELL, IT WAS SWEET OF YOU TO HELP ME BUST OUT!
CAREFUL...

BE QUIET GOING IN! THE DEPUTIES MAY BE DOLTS, BUT THEY'RE NOT DEAF!

STOP WORRYING! 'NIGHT, SWEET-HEART!

ALTERNATE JUROR #7 GETS DRESSED DOWN.
MS. BOOPSTEIN, I REALLY OUGHT TO DISMISS YOU FROM THE JURY RIGHT NOW...

EVEN THOUGH YOU WERE APPARENTLY NOT EXPOSED TO ANY TRIAL PUBLICITY, I AM **EXTREMELY** DISAPPOINT-ED IN YOUR IRRESPON-SIBLE BEHAVIOR!

DO YOU HAVE ANYTHING TO SAY FOR YOURSELF?

YES, YOUR HONOR. I BOUGHT YOU A BELT AT SAKS!
OH... UM... APPROACH THE BENCH.

AS MR. BUTTS RECALLS IT.
SO I'M JUST READING THE NEWS-PAPER, OKAY?
DAILY BLAH
STATES OUT OF CONTROL

SUDDENLY I SEE THE NEWS THAT **STATES** ARE PRESSING CLASS-ACTION SUITS AGAINST TOBACCO COMPANIES! I CAN SCARCELY BELIEVE MY **PEEPERS!**

FRANKLY, I'M STEAMED! THIS IS SUPPOSED TO BE A **CON-SERVATIVE** ERA – WITH **LESS** INTERFERENCE FROM GOV-ERNMENT!
I DECIDE TO **DEMAND** AN EXPLA-NATION!

WHAT'S THE DEAL WITH ALL THE **LAWSUITS?**
I DON'T CONTROL THE COURTS.
YET.

MR. BUTTS RECALLS.
SO I ASK THE SPEAKER, "WHAT'S THE **DEAL**? I THOUGHT YOU PEOPLE WERE GOING TO **CONTAIN** PRODUCT LIABILITY!"
KEEP YOUR **SHIRT** ON!
...HE ADMON-ISHES ME.

WE'RE GETTING TO IT AS FAST AS WE CAN! THE PROBLEM IS THE LAWYERS – THEY **HATE** RE-FORM! TAKE THE FLORIDA SUIT, WHERE THE STATE IS TRYING TO RECOVER $1.4 BILLION IN MED-ICAL COSTS...

KNOW HOW MUCH THE LAW-YERS GET IF THEY WIN? **$350 MILLION! THAT'S** WHY THEY'RE TAKING ON TOBACCO!
YOU GUYS BETTER BE **READY!**

PANICKED, I ENROLL IN LAW SCHOOL!
BUT IT TURNS OUT TO BE **TOO BORING!**

AT FIRST I WORRY MYSELF **SICK** OVER THE FLORIDA CLASS-ACTION SUIT...

THEN SUDDENLY, IT **HITS** ME! THE SUIT IS FOR ONLY $1.4 BILLION! THE TOBACCO COMPANIES MAKE MORE THAN **$50** BILLION IN THE U.S.!
SO EVEN IF WE **LOSE**, WE CAN HANDLE IT! NOW **THAT'S** CAUSE FOR CELEBRATION!

THEN I REMEMBER– THERE ARE 50 STATES!
I BUM MYSELF, TOTALLY.

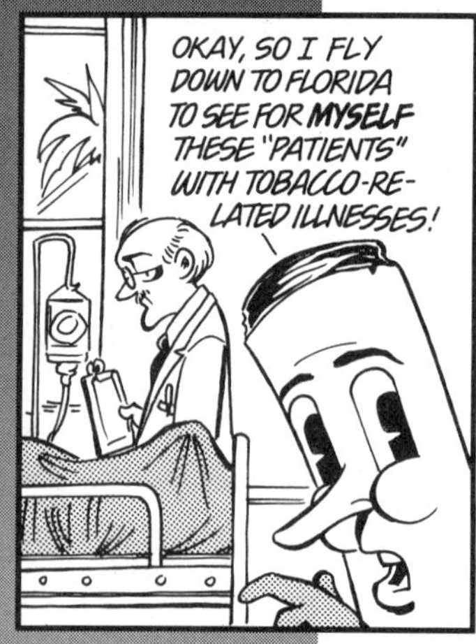
OKAY, SO I FLY DOWN TO FLORIDA TO SEE FOR **MYSELF** THESE "PATIENTS" WITH TOBACCO-RELATED ILLNESSES!

THIS PATIENT HAS EMPHYSEMA. EACH DAY HE'S IN THE HOSPITAL COSTS THE STATE $900. THAT'S WHY WE'RE SUING.
...CLAIMED THE ATTENDING DOCTOR!

LATER, I HAVE A DARK NIGHT OF THE SOUL...
I TAKE A LONG WALK...
I AGONIZE...

...I GET **OVER** IT!
HECK, I'M IN **FLORIDA!**

I DECIDE TO TAKE THE BULL BY THE HORNS! I SET UP AN APPOINTMENT WITH THE **GOVERNOR** HIMSELF!

GOVERNOR, IF YOU DRIVE TOBACCO OUT OF FLORIDA, PEOPLE WILL PUT ON **WEIGHT!** THINK OF THE IMPACT ON YOUR **BEACHES!** AND THE **TOURIST TRADE!** OKAY?

MY **GOD**, SIR! PEOPLE ARE DYING AND YOU SPEAK OF **WEIGHT GAIN?** HAVE YOU NO SHAME, SIR? HAVE YOU FINALLY NO **SHAME?**

I EXTEND MY VISIT TO THINK IT OVER!
WONDER WHAT HE MEANT BY SHAME...

ON THE FACE OF IT, NOT SUCH A HOT WEEK FOR OLD BUTTSIE, RIGHT?
WRONG.

YOU SEE, I SUDDENLY REMEMBERED SOMETHING: WE **NEVER** LOSE LAWSUITS! SINCE 1954, WE'VE WON 800 IN A **ROW!**

SO **WHAT** WAS I WORRIED ABOUT? THE INDUSTRY HAD THINGS UNDER CONTROL! IT WAS TIME FOR ME TO GET BACK TO WHAT **I** DO **BEST!**

AND THAT'S WHY YOU'RE TALKING TO US?
THAT'S RIGHT, SUZY! AND TO KIDS **JUST LIKE** YOU ALL OVER FLORIDA!

AS WE VOTE ON THE NUTRITION PROGRAM THIS WEEK, LET ME REMIND YOU...

THE ISSUE IS NOT WHETHER WE SHOULD HAVE SCHOOL LUNCHES AND BREAKFASTS! NORMAL AMERICAN CHILDREN WILL NOT GO HUNGRY!

THE ISSUE IS WHO DECIDES WHO EATS AND WHO DOESN'T! SHOULD IT BE A FACELESS FEDERAL BUREAUCRAT?
GB Trudeau

NO! IT MUST BE THE CARING, FRONT-LINE PROVIDER!
HONEY! RUN THOSE NUMBERS AGAIN!

WHAT YOU LIBERAL, ELITE MEDIA STILL DON'T GET IS THAT THE AMERICAN PEOPLE VOTED FOR FUNDAMENTAL CHANGE!

THEY WANT TO BE RE-EMPOWERED! THEY'RE TIRED OF BLOATED, UNRESPONSIVE, TOP-DOWN FEDERAL GOVERNMENT!

THEY UNDERSTAND THAT STATE GOVERNMENTS— LEAN, UNCORRUPT, CLOSE TO THE PEOPLE—ARE MUCH MORE LIKELY TO SPEND THEIR MONEY WISELY!

PLEASE, SIR— I'D LIKE SOME MORE KETCHUP.
SORRY, KID, WE'RE BUILDING A NEW PRISON.
GB Trudeau

WITH THIS ANTI-HANDOUT BILL, WHAT WE NORMAL AMERICANS ARE SAYING TO LIBERAL TRAITORS IS: "LOOK, THERE REALLY IS NO FREE LUNCH!"

MR. SPEAKER, YOU TALK ABOUT YOUR BILL LIKE IT'S A FAIT ACCOMPLI! AREN'T YOU CONCERNED ABOUT A POSSIBLE VETO?

YEAH, SHAKIN' IN MY BOOTS! COME ON, CLINTON ISN'T A PLAYER ANYMORE! HE'S IRRELEVANT TO THE PROCESS!
GB Trudeau

OH, YEAH? OH, YEAH?
OOPS... OUT OF INK!

...AND WE'VE SCHEDULED ANOTHER BREAKFAST FOR YOU, SIR...

WE THINK GINGRICH'S ANTI-BREAKFAST BILL IS A WINNER FOR US! THIS COULD BE THE VETO WE'VE BEEN LOOKING FOR!

I KNOW—AND HE WON'T EXPECT IT! HE SAYS I HAVEN'T GOT THE SPINE TO VETO IT! CAN YOU IMAGINE? THE ARROGANCE! HOW DOES **HE** KNOW IF I'VE GOT THE SPINE?

HELL, EVEN **I** DON'T KNOW IF I DO!
I MEAN, I MIGHT.
IT DEPENDS.
GBTrudeau

OKAY, LET'S DO ONE... THIS IS ROLAND HEDLEY. TODAY, IN AN EFFORT TO DRAMATIZE HIS SUPPORT FOR THE FREE BREAKFAST PROGRAM, BILL CLINTON HAS COME TO THIS WASHINGTON AREA SCHOOL...

NO, NO, TOO LONG... I'LL NEED A REWRITE ON THIS...
ROLAND!

YO!
THE PRESIDENT IS **DOWN!** A KID TRIED TO **EAT** HIM!

I'M REALLY SORRY, SIR! I DIDN'T KNOW IT WAS YOU!
NO PROBLEM. JUST A SCRATCH.

LEON, THAT WAS A **VERY** UNPLEASANT EXPERIENCE...

I'M SORRY, MR. PRESIDENT. THE KID WAS JUST HUNGRY. HE DIDN'T RECOGNIZE YOU IN THAT CROWDED CAFETERIA...

IT'S NOT JUST THE KID, LEON...
THERE'S A WHOLE PATTERN OF THIS!

I'M **TIRED** OF BEING EATEN FOR BREAKFAST!
MAYBE IF WE BEEFED UP YOUR DETAIL...
GBTrudeau

GOOD MORNING, FATHER DUKE!
DONUTS

HUH... WHAT? DAMN! DON'T SNEAK UP ON ME LIKE THAT, KID!

IF I'VE TOLD YOU ONCE, I'VE TOLD YOU A THOUSAND TIMES, DON'T... DON'T...

OKAY, WHO ARE YOU?
YOUR FIRST ORPHAN. ARE THOSE YOUR DONUTS?

MAN... I HAVEN'T FELT THIS BAD SINCE NIXON WAS RE-ELECTED...
SORRY I WOKE YOU UP, FATHER.

HOW LONG HAVE YOU BEEN HERE, KID?
ABOUT A WEEK, SIR!

A WEEK?
YUP! I'VE HAD THE BEST TIME!

DAMN! ANOTHER UNBILLABLE WEEK...
LIKE WHEN YOU BLEW UP YOUR CAR! THAT WAS WAY COOL!

HONEY! THERE'S SOME KID DOWNSTAIRS!
YES, SIR. HIS NAME'S STEWART. HE'S OUR FIRST RE-FERRAL.

REFERRAL? REFERRAL FOR WHAT? I HATE KIDS!
UM... YOU'VE STARTED AN ORPHANAGE, SIR. DON'T YOU REMEM-BER?

IT'S THAT ASIAN SENSE OF HUMOR! I'LL NEVER GET USED TO IT!
IT'S NO JOKE, SIR. IT'S A 24-BED UNIT.

NO WAY I SET UP AN ORPHANAGE, HONEY! I DESPISE CHILDREN!
SEE FOR YOURSELF, SIR...

Nothin' but Orphans Inc.

AN ANGLE... I MUST'VE HAD AN ANGLE...
MAYBE YOU WERE TRYING TO CYNICALLY EXPLOIT AN UGLY NEW POLITICAL MOOD FOR YOUR OWN GAIN.
GB Trudeau

THAT'S IT! I REMEMBER NOW!
KIND OF LIKE THE SUN COMING OUT, ISN'T IT, SIR?

HEY, FATHER DUKE, THE GARAGE SEEMED KIND OF MESSY, SO I PICKED IT UP. OKAY?

YEAH, FINE, KID.
I LIKE THIS HOME SO MUCH BETTER THAN MY LAST ONE! THEY MADE ME LEAVE BECAUSE I SET FIRE TO THE CARPET.

BEFORE THAT, I DROPPED MY FOSTER FATHER'S GOLF CLUBS OFF A BRIDGE. AND BEFORE THAT I TIED UP BOTH MY FOSTER PARENTS IN BED AND SPRAY-PAINTED THEM!
GB Trudeau

PSST, SIR! STEWART'S DESPERATE FOR ATTENTION.
NO KIDDING.
SO. WANNA PLAY BALL?

THAT WAS THE LADY FROM THE AGENCY, SIR. SHE'S COMING OUT THIS AFTERNOON TO DISCUSS SOME MORE REFERRALS WITH YOU...

SORRY, HONEY. NO CAN DO. I'M GOING ON A LITTLE TRIP.

A TRIP? WHEN?
ACTUALLY, IT'S ALREADY BEGUN.
GB Trudeau

I'VE HAD IT WITH YOU, SIR!
LAST TIME. PROMISE.

...AND LITTLE JESSICA COMES TO US FROM LEAD-VILLE!

WITH HER ARRIVAL, WE NOW HAVE 21 OF OUR 24 BEDS OCCUPIED!

MY GOD... WHAT A NIGHT-MARE!
WHAT DO YOU MEAN, SIR?
©B Trudeau

LOOK AT IT FROM MY PERSPECTIVE, HONEY...
I CAN'T, SIR. IT'S ILLEGAL.

HERE'S HOW IT BREAKS DOWN, SIR. TEN OF OUR KIDS ARE BOYS, ELEVEN ARE GIRLS. WE'VE GOT NINE WHITES, SIX BLACKS...

...FOUR HISPANICS AND TWO ASIANS! OUR ORPHANAGE IS THE VERY **MODEL** OF DIVERSITY!

WELL, GREAT! THAT'S JUST **GREAT!**
WHAT'S WRONG, SIR? YOU SOUND PEEVED...
©B Trudeau

DAMMIT, HONEY! YOU **KNOW** I'M RACIST!
YES, SIR. THIS IS YOUR CHANCE TO WORK ON IT.

HEY, **BALDY!** WHAT'S THE DEAL ON MY BED? IT'S GOT LUMPS THE SIZE OF **GRAPEFRUIT!**

GET ME A NEW MATTRESS OR I'LL HAVE MY CASE WORKER COME OUT HERE AND RIP YOUR **LUNGS** OUT, **OKAY?**
UH... SURE, KID.

©B Trudeau

HONEY, IS IT JUST ME, OR DOES THAT KID LOOK LIKE...
HIS MOTHER'S A LOCAL STRIP-PER, SIR. RING ANY BELLS?

THERE'S SOMETHING ABOUT THAT KID, HONEY...
YES, SIR. HE'S A DEAD RINGER FOR YOU.

HIS NAME'S EARL. HIS MOTHER'S A LOCAL STRIPPER WITH A HISTORY OF DRUG PROBLEMS...

THAT MEANS NOTHING. A MILLION PEOPLE FIT THAT DESCRIPTION!
QUITE RIGHT, SIR! ONLY A DNA TEST CAN TELL. THAT'S WHY LAST WEEK, WHEN YOU WERE UNCONSCIOUS, I TOOK THE LIBERTY OF... OF...

OF WHAT? OF WHAT?
I SENT ONE OF YOUR WARTS OFF TO THE LAB. JUST TO BE SURE.

YOU TOOK A TISSUE SAMPLE FROM ME?
YES, SIR. AND THE DOCTOR GOT ONE FROM LITTLE EARL.

A DNA TEST IS THE ONLY WAY TO TELL IF HE'S YOUR SON. IN THIS AGE OF PERSONAL RESPONSIBILITY, I KNEW YOU'D WANT TO KNOW!

ARE YOU INSANE? WHY WOULD I WANT TO KNOW? I DO NOT WANT TO KNOW!
THE RESULTS WERE CONCLUSIVE. HE'S YOURS.

I DIDN'T HEAR THAT! I DID NOT HEAR THAT!
SHALL I TELL HIM, SIR, OR WILL YOU?

"...AND OUR DNA ANALYSIS PROVES CONCLUSIVELY THAT THE CHILD EARL IS MR. DUKE'S SON."

I... I... DON'T BELIEVE THIS...
WELL, I CAN UNDERSTAND YOUR SHOCK, SIR...

AFTER MANY, MANY YEARS OF HARD, IRRESPONSIBLE LIVING, IT'S THE FIRST TIME YOU'VE PRODUCED A CHILD!

NO... NO... IT'S THE FIRST TIME ANYONE'S PROVED IT!
IT MUST BE A JOYOUS MOMENT, SIR.

A FATHER AND SON MEET FOR THE FIRST TIME.
DUKE'S GOING OVER TO TELL LITTLE EARL...

IT'S TOO HEARTBREAKING. I CAN'T BEAR TO WATCH...

NEITHER CAN WE. LET'S GO BACK TO THE O.J. TRIAL.
AND THAT'S WHEN YOU STARTED BARKING?
ARF!

NEVER MIND.
YEAH, RIGHT. AND MY MOTHER'S DOLLY PARTON.
LOOK, KID, I'M NOT EXACTLY THRILLED MYSELF.

YOU'RE NOT MY FATHER. I DON'T HAVE A FATHER.
LOOK, I DON'T LIKE THE IDEA ANY MORE THAN YOU, KID...

UNFORTUNATELY, THE DNA TEST RESULTS CONFIRM IT. SEE FOR YOURSELF.

OKAY, CAN I HAVE MY ALLOW-ANCE?
NO. THIS IS AN ORPHANAGE. I CAN'T PLAY FAVORITES.

LOOK, KID, YOU'VE GOT EVERY RIGHT TO HATE ME. HELL, I WOULDN'T BLAME YOU IF YOU JUST TOOK OFF, NEVER TO RETURN!

YOU'D LIKE THAT, WOULDN'T YOU, "DAD"?
FRANKLY, YES. I COULD USE THE BED. THE FEDS WON'T PAY ME TO TAKE CARE OF MY OWN KID.

WELL, FORGET IT. I'VE GOT TOO MUCH IN-VESTED HERE.
WHAT ARE YOU TALKING ABOUT?

I ALREADY GOT LOANS OUT TO FOUR KIDS.
YOU'RE SHARKING? YOU'RE SHARK-ING IN MY ORPHANAGE?

LOOK, KID, I JUST THINK YOU'D BE MORE COMFORTABLE IN SOME OTHER SETTING THAN A CROWDED ORPHANAGE...

UH-HUH. IF YOU'RE SO CONCERNED ABOUT MY WELFARE, WHY DID YOU LEAVE MY MOTHER?

IT'S VERY COMPLICATED, KID... YOUR MOTHER AND I JUST COULDN'T... WELL... SHE WAS VERY... UM... SHE WAS... UM...

WHO'S YOUR MOTHER AGAIN?
AND PEOPLE WONDER WHY I SET FIRES.
GBTrudeau

SIR! HOW ARE YOU AND LITTLE EARL HITTING IT OFF?

YOU DON'T WANT TO KNOW.
ACTUALLY, I DO, SIR. I CARE ABOUT BOTH OF YOU.
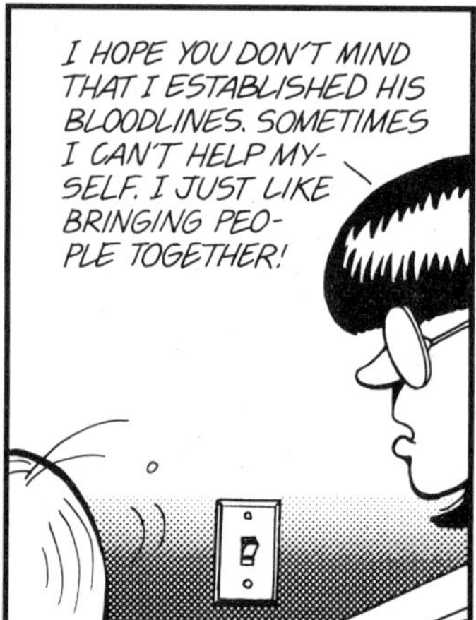
I HOPE YOU DON'T MIND THAT I ESTABLISHED HIS BLOODLINES. SOMETIMES I CAN'T HELP MYSELF. I JUST LIKE BRINGING PEOPLE TOGETHER!

THANK YOU, JENNY JONES. WHERE'S THAT GUNNY-SACK?
UM... WHY?
GBTrudeau

AS THE YEARS WENT BY, LITTLE EARL GREW UP STRAIGHT AND STRONG.
HEY, DAD! I NAILED MY SAT'S! JUST NAILED 'EM!
UH-HUH...

HEY, POP! I MADE IT INTO HARVARD LAW SCHOOL!
GREAT...

POPS! I JUST SCORED $350 MILLION IN A HOSTILE TAKEOVER!
REALLY?

NO, NOT REALLY.
HEY, DAD! I JUST PUT A SQUIRREL IN THE MICROWAVE!
MY GOD... HE'S STILL HERE...
GBTrudeau

B.D.? IT'S SID! LOOKS LIKE OUR LITTLE GIRL'S ON THE FAST TRACK!
WHAT DO YOU MEAN?

THE JURY! THEY'RE DROPPING LIKE FLIES! NO WAY THEY'RE NOT GOING TO USE ALL THE ALTERNATES!

BOOPSIE'S GOING TO BE AN O.J. JUROR! I GUARANTEE IT! I'D BET MY NEW MER-CEDES ON IT!

HI. I GOT BOOTED.
YOU'RE ON. I'LL SEND HER OVER FOR THE KEYS.

CAN YOU BE-LIEVE IT? I INVESTED FOUR MONTHS OF MY LIFE IN THAT TRIAL!
HOW'D YOU GET DIS-MISSED?

IT WASN'T ME! SOMETHING CAME OUT ABOUT HUNK-RA'S PAST!
OH, YEAH? WHAT?

IT WAS NOTHING! OF NO CON-SEQUENCE!
UH-HUH.

I BEHEADED MY FIFTH WIFE! BIG DEAL!
YOU DIDN'T MEN-TION THAT ON THE QUESTION-NAIRE?

I DUNNO, B.D., MAYBE IT'S JUST AS WELL THAT I WAS DISMISSED...
I'M NOT SURE HOW MUCH MORE OF THAT SEQUESTRA-TION I COULD HAVE TAKEN. IT WAS BECOMING UNBEAR-ABLE.

I CAN'T TELL YOU HOW GOOD IT FEELS TO BE HOME. AT LAST OUR LIVES CAN GET BACK TO NORMAL!

SO WHY AREN'T YOU AT WORK?
GULF WAR SYN-DROME.

B.D., ARE YOU SURE IT'S THE GULF WAR SYNDROME? WHAT ARE YOUR SYMPTOMS?

MOSTLY FATIGUE. I'VE HAD IT OFF AND ON EVER SINCE THE WAR. BUT NOW IT'S SO BAD, I'M TOO TIRED TO GO TO WORK!

WHOA ... YOU KNOW, NOW THAT YOU MENTION IT...
WHAT IS IT, ZONK?
©B Trudeau

I HAVEN'T FELT LIKE WORKING SINCE THE WAR, EITHER!
MAYBE YOU SHOULD GO IN TOGETHER.

B.D., HOW LONG HAVE YOU BEEN TOO TIRED TO GO TO WORK?
I DUNNO. ABOUT A WEEK.

HAVE YOU HAD ANY OTHER SYMPTOMS?
NOTHING MUCH. JUST SOME SHORT-TERM MEMORY LOSS AND MOOD SWINGS.

WHAT? B.D., THAT'S **SERIOUS!**

I MEAN, MEMORY LOSS AND MOOD SWINGS ARE...
MOOD SWINGS? WHO SAID ANYTHING ABOUT **MOOD SWINGS?**
©B Trudeau
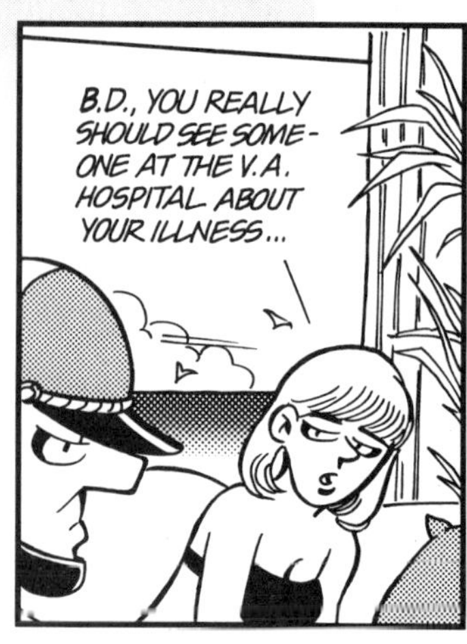
B.D., YOU REALLY SHOULD SEE SOMEONE AT THE V.A. HOSPITAL ABOUT YOUR ILLNESS...

I ALREADY WENT IN—LAST YEAR. NO ONE BELIEVED ME. THE DOCTOR TOLD ME IT WAS ALL IN MY HEAD.

BESIDES, I'M AFRAID IF I GO BACK IN, THEY'LL... THEY'LL...
THEY'LL WHAT?
©B Trudeau

THEY'LL TRY TO CUT MY HELMET OFF AGAIN!
YOU BIG BABY! JUST ASK FOR A LOCAL.

SIR, IN THE WAKE OF THE OKLAHOMA TRAGEDY, A LOT OF PEOPLE WOULD LIKE TO HEAR THE VOLUME TURNED DOWN ON HATE RADIO...

OH, YEAH? WELL, WHY DON'T THEY JUST **SHRED** THE CONSTITUTION WHILE THEY'RE AT IT!

UGLY, TOXIC, ANTI-GOVERNMENT RHETORIC IS OUR GOD-GIVEN **RIGHT!** AND I DEEPLY RESENT THIS **DESPICABLE** ATTEMPT TO LINK ME TO THE CURRENT EXPLOSIVE MOOD!

SO YOU WON'T BE TAKING A HARD LOOK AT YOURSELF?
OF **COURSE** NOT! WHAT DO YOU MEAN?
GB Trudeau

MR. SPEAKER, MOST AMERICANS SEEM TO AGREE WITH THE PRESIDENT THAT MAYBE IT'S TIME WE RESTORED A LITTLE CIVILITY TO PUBLIC DISCOURSE...

RIGHT! AND WHO'S GOING TO DECIDE WHAT'S CIVIL—THAT SNIVELING LIBERAL **DEGENERATE?**

CLINTON'S ATTEMPT TO "HEAL" BY CONDEMNING HATE RADIO WAS A **COWARDLY** ATTACK ON OUR BASIC FREEDOMS, ON THE CONSTITUTION **ITSELF!**

AND HIS MOMENT OF SILENCE?
MORE GOVERNMENT INTRUSION!
GB Trudeau

SIR, YOU'RE STILL GETTING KILLED OUT THERE FOR TAKING ON HATE RADIO...
I AM?

BUT I WASN'T TALKING ABOUT SPECIFIC RADIO SHOWS! I JUST MEANT PUBLIC DISCOURSE IN **GENERAL**...

BUT NOBODY BELIEVED THAT, SIR! AS LONG AS YOU'RE BEING PILLORIED ANYWAY, YOU MIGHT AS WELL TAKE CREDIT FOR WHAT WAS A **VERY** PRINCIPLED STAND!

HEY... IT **WAS,** WASN'T IT?
WELL, I SUPPOSE I COULD TEST THE WATERS...
GB Trudeau

HI, THIS IS BILL CLINTON CALLING!

I JUST WANTED TO CLARIFY MY POSITION ON HATE RADIO...

I DEPLORE IT! I THINK IT HAS CONTRIBUTED TO THE POISONOUS ANTI-GOVERNMENT MOOD IN THIS COUNTRY...
©B Trudeau

DO YOU THINK IT'S REALLY HIM?
DON'T YOU HAVE CALLER I.D.?

ANYWAY, I REALLY DID MEAN TO COME OUT AGAINST HATE RADIO. THERE'S BEEN SOME CONFUSION THERE.

MR. PRESIDENT, WHEN YOU SAY "HATE RADIO," ARE YOU REFERRING TO CONSERVATIVE, CALL-IN, TALK-RADIO SHOWS?

ABSOLUTELY, UNEQUIVOCALLY, YES!
HE SAYS YES.
IT CAN'T BE CLINTON!

...EXCEPT FOR RUSH LIMBAUGH, OLIVER NORTH, BOB GRANT, G. GORDON...
IT'S HIM.
©B Trudeau

...I'M ALSO NOT REFERRING TO THE BLANQUITA CULLUM SHOW!

BUT MR. PRESIDENT— YOU CLAIM THAT YOU'RE CONDEMNING HATE TALK RADIO...

...BUT YOU'VE JUST EXEMPTED EVERY MAJOR RIGHT-WING RADIO SHOW IN THE COUNTRY!

WHEW!
WELL, THAT'S BECAUSE I'M HEALER-IN-CHIEF!
©B Trudeau

O.J. CITY... CENTER OF THE UNIVERSE...

...LOCUS OF BOOK DEALS!

NATIONAL DESK!
HEY, BOSS, IT'S RICK.

OUR MAN IN O.J. CITY! TELL ME SOMETHING I DIDN'T READ ON THE WIRES YESTERDAY!
IF YOU INSIST...

ONE OF MY SOURCES AT THE JAILHOUSE BROUGHT ME SOMETHING MIND-BOGGLING LAST NIGHT...
ATTENTION: THIS IS A TEST OF THE EMERGENCY O.J. BULLETIN SYSTEM. THIS IS ONLY A TEST.
ROLAND HEDLEY
HAD THIS BEEN AN ACTUAL EMERGENCY BULLETIN, YOU WOULD HAVE RECEIVED DETAILS OF A BREAKING DEVELOPMENT IN THE O.J. SIMPSON CASE.
ROLAND HEDLEY

NOW BACK TO OUR REGULARLY SCHEDULED STORY LINE.
ROLAND HEDLEY

SORRY, RICK. THAT'S TOO HOT FOR US, TOO EXPLOSIVE.
I WAS AFRAID OF THAT.

UH-OH... HERE THEY COME...

BETTER LOOK BUSY...

OKAY, THERE'S BEEN A LOT OF MEAN-SPIRITED TALK LATELY ABOUT "NEWTOIDS..."

...MEANING, FRESHMEN REPUBLICANS WHO SUPPOSEDLY SUPPORT MY EVERY PROPOSAL WITH BLIND FEALTY!

WELL, IT'S HOGWASH! THE AMERICAN PEOPLE VOTED FOR REPRESENTATIVES WHO WOULD ANSWER TO THEM, NOT TO ME!

NOW, IF SOME MEMBERS OF THE NEW CLASS AREN'T QUITE UP TO SPEED ON THE ISSUES, WELL, THAT'S UNDERSTANDABLE...

AND IN THAT CASE, IT JUST MAKES SENSE TO FOLLOW THE HANDY CHECK-OFF LIST OF RECOMMENDED VOTES PROVIDED TO YOU BY THIS OFFICE, DOESN'T IT?

YES, SIR!!
GOOD! GET BACK TO WORK!
GB Trudeau

I'LL TAKE A LIGHT CAPPUCCINO, HALF DE-CAF, WITH A SPLASH OF SWEET ESPRESSO!

THAT'S IMPRESSIVE, BERNIE. WHERE'D YOU LEARN TO ORDER COFFEE LIKE THAT?
THE GREAT NORTHWEST.

VICE PRESIDENT? WOW! BERNIE, YOU'VE REALLY COME INTO YOUR OWN!
NOT BAD FOR THE ORIGINAL COMPUTER GEEK, HUH?

WHEN I THINK OF THE RIDICULE I ENDURED! DO YOU KNOW I OWN AN INTEREST IN A PROGRAM I DEVELOPED AS A LARK 20 YEARS AGO?

WHICH ONE?
REMEMBER THAT SCHTICK I USED TO DO THAT IRRITATED YOU SO—I CALLED IT HALLUCINATIVE IMAGING?

HALLUCINATIVE IMAGING? HMM... NO, CAN'T SAY THAT I...
POOF!

REMEMBER NOW?

MORPHING? YOU OWN A PIECE OF MORPHING?
15%.
I NOW DRIVE A LEXUS.
©B Trudeau

Mike: Isn't Capt. Janeway's expertise in temporal mechanics?
Kate: I'll check, Mike.
TAP! TAP! TAP!

I'LL JUST PUT MY LIFE ON HOLD UNTIL SHE GETS BACK TO ME...

Kate: IMHO, Chakotay is the most compelling First Officer since Spock.
Mike: Same with Janeway and Kirk.
TAP! TAP!

Cliff: Anyone catch the quarter singularity repeat last night?

Mike: Yeah, I did. Sick of the villain being another spatial phenomenon.
TAP! TAP!

Ted: I agree. Let Trek be Trek. More Klingons!
Cliff: Right on, Ted. Voyager hasn't cut it, characterwise, since episode six, BTW.

Kate: 'Bye, guys. Gotta go to work.
Mike: Work?
TAP! TAP!

OH, NO...
MOMMY! DADDY STAYED UP ALL NIGHT AGAIN!

YOU'LL BE TELLING THE TRUTH, WON'T YOU, SIR?

WHAT KIND OF QUESTION IS THAT, HONEY? I'M HURT.
IS THAT A YES, SIR?

...AND AS YOU CAN SEE FROM OUR FIGURES, CON-GRESSWOMAN, "NOTHIN' BUT ORPHANS" IS THE MOST COST-EFFECTIVE DUMPING GROUND NOW DOING BUSINESS!

WE ORIGINALLY PROPOSED TO SHELTER THESE KIDS FOR $20,000 A POP, BUT BY DOING SOME HARD-EYED COST CUTTING, WE NOW THINK WE CAN DO THE JOB FOR $19,500 PER!

THAT'S ALL VERY WELL, DEAR MAN, BUT I STILL DON'T SEE ANYTHING IN YOUR RESUME THAT SUGGESTS YOU'RE UP TO THE JOB...

THERE ARE VAGUE REFERENCES TO "SERVICE" IN VARIOUS PLACES ABROAD, BUT IT'S ALL VERY MYSTERIOUS. EXACTLY WHAT QUALIFICATIONS **DO** YOU HAVE, FATHER DUKE?

SIR? THE LADY ASKED YOU A DIRECT...
OKAY, $15,000 A KID, BUT IT'S GOTTA BE A BLOCK GRANT!

SURE IS QUIET IN THERE...

COULD ACTUAL STUDYING BE TAKING PLACE?

A·B
C·D
E
F·G
I·J
K·L
HISTORY PAPER TIME...

"Louisiana Purchase (1803): The purchase of the vast Louisiana Territory from France, initiated by Thomas Jefferson."

"The purchased area, which extended from the Mississippi to the Rocky Mountains, doubled the size of the United States."

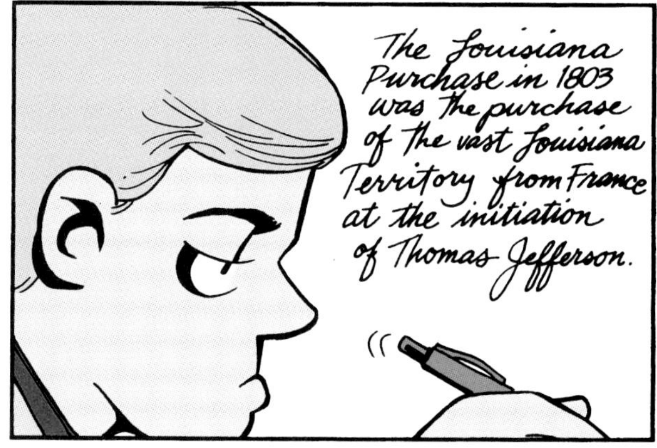
The Louisiana Purchase in 1803 was the purchase of the vast Louisiana Territory from France at the initiation of Thomas Jefferson.

The area that was purchased extended from the Mississippi to the Rockies and doubled the size of the United States.

MY... WHAT A DRAMATIC IMPROVEMENT IN OUR WRITING.
THANKS.

TODAY PHIL GRAMM DISMISSED BOB DOLE'S WAR WOUND...

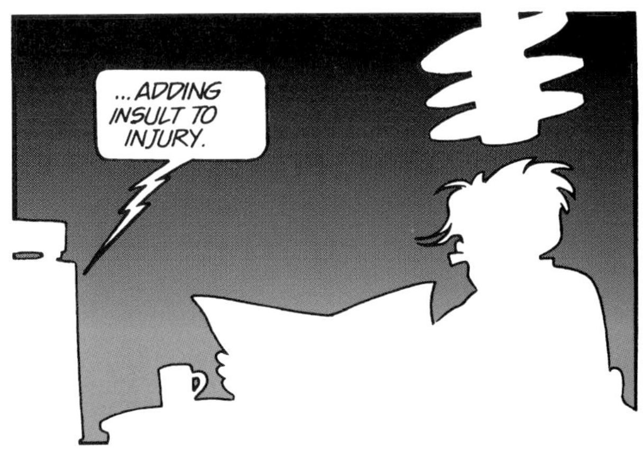
...ADDING INSULT TO INJURY.

HI, MY NAME'S BOB DOLE, AND I'D LIKE TO TALK TO YOU TO-NIGHT ABOUT MY OLD WAR WOUND.

YOU KNOW, THERE USED TO BE A TIME IN AMERICA WHEN HEROES WERE MODEST. A REAL WAR HERO ALWAYS SHRUGGED OFF HIS HEROICS. HE WAS JUST GRATEFUL TO BE ALIVE, HUM-BLED BY GOD'S MERCY...

I MYSELF HAVE ALWAYS TRIED TO BEAR MY INJURY WITH DIGNITY. BUT GEORGE BUSH CHANGED THINGS FOREVER WHEN HE OR-DERED UP A WAR-HERO VIDEO DURING THE 1988 CAMPAIGN.

TODAY A WAR WOUND GIVES YOU A CRITICAL EDGE. FAR FROM BEING A BAD MEMORY FROM THE DISTANT PAST, A WORLD WAR II INJURY IS A CHERISHED PERSONAL SYM-BOL, A BADGE OF HONOR AND SACRIFICE.

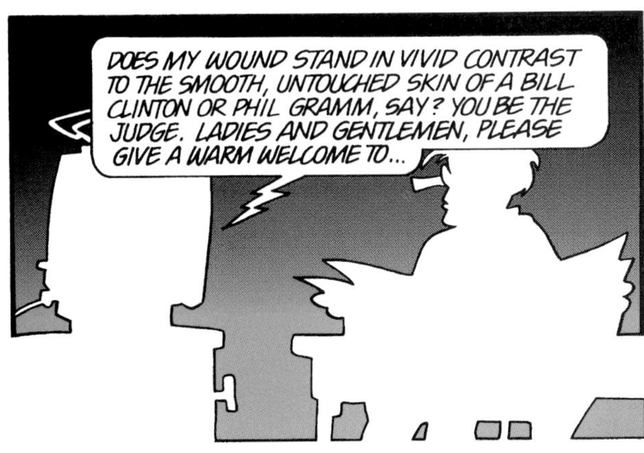
DOES MY WOUND STAND IN VIVID CONTRAST TO THE SMOOTH, UNTOUCHED SKIN OF A BILL CLINTON OR PHIL GRAMM, SAY? YOU BE THE JUDGE. LADIES AND GENTLEMEN, PLEASE GIVE A WARM WELCOME TO...

...MY OLD WAR WOUND!
THANK YOU, BOB. THANK YOU. I'M PROUD TO BE A POLITICAL ASSET.

INVOICE

____________, 19____
DATE

To: Dr. ________________________
NAME
STREET
CITY STATE ZIP

My appointment was at :

I was actually seen at :

For unrecoverable hours wasted in your waiting room
@ $ per hour $
tax $
total $

Please remit payment to:

NAME
STREET
CITY STATE ZIP

MY LOVE! MY SWEET BO PEEP!

I HOPE SHE APPRECIATES THIS...
TAP! TAP!

WELL, I GUESS WE BETTER GET STARTED. MY NAME IS JEREMY CAVENDISH, AND I'M A LOCAL MAN...

FIRST OF ALL, I WANT TO THANK SENATOR ALFONSE D'AMATO FOR THE COURAGE HE SHOWED IN PUBLICLY ANNOUNCING HE WAS GOING STEADY. WITHOUT HIS EXAMPLE, ODDS ARE I WOULDN'T EVEN **BE** HERE TODAY!

THE SENATOR HAS INSPIRED ME TO GO PUBLIC AND DE-CLARE MY OWN INTENTIONS IN REGARDS TO ANOTHER GREAT PUBLIC FIGURE — **MRS. LACEY DAVENPORT**!

MRS. D IS A FAIRY TALE COME TRUE! SHE IS MY CURDS AND WHEY, AND I AM HER THIRD LITTLE PIG!
I WOULD DIE TO CALL HER MY BETROTHED, IDEALLY BEFORE THE SEASON STARTS AT NEWPORT!

UNFORTUNATELY, I GET ON HER NERVES. AT LEAST THAT'S WHAT CONSUELA, HER MAID, TELLS ME...
YES, YOU UP FRONT — YOU HAVE A QUESTION?

YEAH, I WAS TOLD THERE'D BE REFRESH-MENTS.
NO TIME! YOU'RE ON DEADLINE!
©B Trudeau

IT'S JUST TOO EERIE...

IT CAN'T BE A CO-INCIDENCE!

YOU'RE LOOKIN' BUMMED TODAY, DUDE. WHAT'S UP?
I DON'T KNOW, CORNELL. IT'S JUST THIS CREEPY FEELING I'VE HAD ABOUT MY LIFE LATELY...

YOUR LIFE? WHAT'S WRONG WITH YOUR LIFE?
WELL, CHECK IT OUT. I'M A SURFER, RIGHT? WITH BITCHIN' HAIR, RIGHT?

TOTALLY.
AND WHERE DO I LIVE?

WHERE DO YOU LIVE? IN SOUTHERN CALIFORNIA, MAN.
SURE, BUT WITH WHO? AN EX-FOOTBALL PLAYER AND HIS BLOND WIFE! AND AS WHAT? AS A PERMANENT HOUSEGUEST!

WHERE'RE YOU GOING WITH THIS, MAN?
DON'T YOU SEE? IT COULD HAVE BEEN ME! I COULD HAVE BEEN KATO KAELIN!

WHOA... MAYBE YOU ARE, DUDE! LIKE, IN A PARALLEL LIFE!
NO, NO, IT'S A SIGN, CORNELL! I'VE GOT TO MAKE A CHANGE!

OH, NO...

D'AMATO'S DONE IT AGAIN!
NEW YORK POS

THANK YOU FOR CALLING THE OFFICE OF SENATOR AL D'AMATO. WE CERTAINLY APPRECIATE YOUR CALL.

IF YOU ARE CALLING TO MAKE A CONTRIBUTION, PRESS ONE. IF YOU ARE CALLING TO REPORT A POTHOLE, PRESS TWO.

IF YOU WOULD LIKE TO HEAR WHY WHITEWATER IS WORSE THAN ANY OF SENATOR D'AMATO'S SCANDALS, PRESS THREE.

IF YOU WOULD LIKE TO HEAR A POLISH JOKE, PRESS FOUR. FOR AN ASIAN JOKE, PRESS FIVE. FOR A GREAT JOKE ABOUT BLACK PEOPLE, PRESS SIX.

IF YOU WISH TO DISCUSS ANY SUBSTANTIVE ISSUE, CALL SOME-ONE WHO CARES. IF YOU WISH TO LEAVE A MESSAGE, SPEAK WHEN YOU HEAR THE BEEP.
BEEP!

UH... YEAH. I'D LIKE TO LEAVE A MES-SAGE FOR SENATOR D'AMATO...
SPEAKING!
HA! HA! GOTCHA! THE OLD VOICE MAIL GAG!
SOLLY, CHOLLY! YUK! YUK!

AH... THAT WAS GREAT...

NOTHIN' LIKE A GOOD BREAKFAST TO START THE DAY!

OKAY, SON, LET'S SEE HOW CLOSELY YOU'VE BEEN PAYING ATTENTION. HERE'S THE SET-UP: YOU'RE LYING IN BED WHEN YOU HEAR A NOISE. WHAT DO YOU DO?

I LEAP OUT OF BED, AND I GRAB MY PIECE FROM THE NIGHTSTAND.

I DROP INTO A CROUCH AND EMPTY A FULL CLIP IN THE DI-RECTION OF THE NOISE!
CLIK! CLIK!
CLIK!
CLIK! CLIK!
CLIK!

RIGHT, BUT YOU MADE ONE BIG MISTAKE, DIDN'T YOU? WHAT SAFETY RULE DID YOU BREAK?
SAFETY RULE?

THINK, BOY, **THINK!** THIS IS **IMPORTANT!**
UM... LET'S SEE...

YOU NEVER, **EVER** LEAVE YOUR WEA-PON UNLOADED!
OH, RIGHT... I KNEW THAT...

HMM... WHO SHOULD I CHAT WITH, ANDREA OR JENNIFER?

JENNIFER SOUNDS HOTTER...
TAP! TAP!

I'LL BE THERE IN A MINUTE, J.J.–I'M IN THE MIDDLE OF A CONVERSATION.
AND A MIGHTY IMPORT-ANT ONE, TOO, I'M GUESSING.
TAP! TAP!

SEE, THIS IS ONE REASON WHY WOMEN DON'T USE THE NET. WE HAVE A HARD TIME THINKING OF LITTLE POSTS BETWEEN STRANGERS AS ACTUAL CONVERSATIONS.

J.J., THAT'S RIDICULOUS. THERE ARE PLENTY OF WOMEN ON THE NET.
WHERE? IN THE SINGLES CHAT GROUPS?

WELL, AMONG OTHER PLACES, SURE.
OH, RIGHT, MIKE! WOMEN JUST LOVE TO SPEND HOURS TALKING DIRTY TO ADOLESCENT, GET-A-LIFE NET-HEADS!
GIVE ME A BREAK!

Jennifer: You're a woman, aren't you?
Um...why?
TAP! TAP! TAP!

HMM... I'M IN THE MOOD FOR A TOUCH O' TRASH...

OPRAH LOOKS GOOD...

OKAY, LET ME SEE IF I CAN WRAP THIS UP...

SHERRI, YOU SAY YOU WERE IN LOVE WITH COR-NELL, YOUR FATHER'S BOYFRIEND, UNTIL YOU FOUND OUT HE WAS AL-SO SEEING YOUR SISTER.
RIGHT.

AND CORNELL, YOU SAY YOU COULDN'T HELP IT, THAT YOUR MOTHER ANGIE BEAT YOU AND STOPPED SLEEPING WITH YOU WHEN SHE LEARNED ABOUT YOUR SEX ADDICTION.
YEAH.

AND ANGIE, AFTER YOU FOUND YOUR SON CHEAT-ING ON YOU, YOU PAID HIM BACK BY BACKING OVER SHERRI'S SISTER.
THE TRAMP **DESERVED** IT!

OKAY, NOW, LET ME ASK YOU ALL THIS—WHY DID YOU DECIDE TO GO PUB-LIC, DEGRADING YOUR-SELVES IN FRONT OF THIS AUDIENCE AND MILLIONS OF VIEWERS?
©B Trudeau

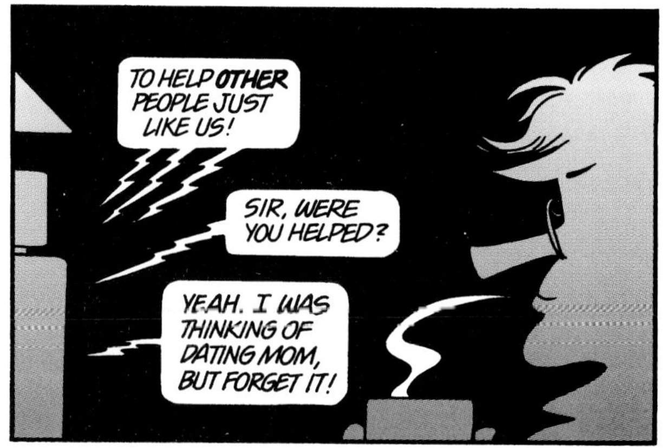
TO HELP **OTHER** PEOPLE JUST LIKE US!
SIR, WERE YOU HELPED?
YEAH. I WAS THINKING OF DATING MOM, BUT FORGET IT!

HMM... I DON'T SEEM TO BE GETTING ANY POSTINGS...

I'VE GOT TO GET MY OWN WEB SITE— AND FAST!

Are you still there, sweet husband?
TAP! TAP! TAP!

Affirmative. Just a keystroke away. Almost as fast as thought itself.
LIBRA
MON-FRI
TAP! TAP!

You've made me a believer, El. I don't know how we ever got by without PC's!
TAP! TAP! TAP!

So true! Ye gods, these machines are miraculous! Who knew the future would be so sweet?
TAP! TAP! TAP!

Not me!
Well, time to go, my love.
TAP! TAP!

Why? They kicking us out?
No, my carpal tunnel's acting up...
HOURS
5:00
TAP! TAP!
TAP! TAP!

NO WAY N.P.R. IS GOING TO SURVIVE THE BUDGET AX ...

MAYBE IF WE SWITCHED TO A RIGHT-WING FORMAT...

WE'RE BACK, AND OUR NEXT GUEST IS MARVIN PICCALO, CELEBRATED AUTHOR OF "OUT OF THE CLOSET AT 40"!

THIS, OF COURSE, IS A SUBJECT DEAR TO MY HEART. COMING TO TERMS WITH GAYNESS AT MID-LIFE IS SOMETHING THAT...
ACTUALLY, MARK, I'M BACK IN THE CLOSET NOW.

YOU'RE WHAT?
IT WASN'T WORTH THE HASSLE...

... THE DISCRIMINATION, THE BIGOTRY, THE PROBLEMS WITH FAMILY—IT WAS ALL MORE THAN I COULD HANDLE. SO I DECIDED TO GO BACK TO LIVING A LIE. I'M EVEN DATING WOMEN AGAIN.

DATING WOMEN?
RIGHT.

LUCKY THEM.
YOU'D BE SURPRISED. A LOT OF GIRLS **GO** FOR A GUY WHO'S WELL-BEHAVED.
©B Trudeau

HEY, HONEY, IT'S ZONKER! JUST CALLING IN TO SEE HOW UNCLE DUKE IS TAKING TO FATHERHOOD...

HE'S DOING SURPRISINGLY WELL, SIR. HE'S REALLY COME AROUND ON IT...

HE NOW SAYS HE WANTS TO TEACH LITTLE EARL ALL THE CHILDHOOD GAMES HIS FATHER NEVER HAD TIME TO TEACH HIM!

AND IF I WIN THE HAND?
THEN **SHE** HAS TO REMOVE AN ARTICLE OF CLOTHING.

HOLD DOWN THE FORT, HONEY. THE KID AND I ARE GOING INTO TOWN...

YOU'RE TAKING LITTLE EARL ON AN OUTING, SIR?
YUP. IT'S TIME FOR A LITTLE MALE BONDING...
CLIK!

I THOUGHT I'D TAKE HIM IN FOR HIS FIRST TATTOO— MY TREAT!
SIR! HE'S NINE YEARS **OLD!**
I KNOW. SO MUCH PARENTING, SO LITTLE TIME.
C'MON, DAD! WE'LL BE LATE FOR MY APPOINTMENT!

THIS IS IT, SON—THE LEGENDARY **ASPEN BODY ARTS!**
BE RIGHT WITH YOU! WE'RE STERILIZING THE NEEDLES.

NEEDLES? NOBODY SAID ANYTHING ABOUT **NEEDLES!** THAT'S IT—I'M OUTA HERE!
THE HELL YOU ARE...

EARL, GETTING YOUR FIRST TATTOO IS AN IMPORTANT RITE OF MANHOOD! DO YOU THINK I RAISED YOU TO BE A **WIMP?**

WHO **KNOWS?** YOU'VE ONLY BEEN RAISING ME FOR TEN MINUTES!
KID, I'M LOSING FACE HERE...
WHY DON'T YOU GIRLS SLEEP ON IT?

I CAN'T **BELIEVE** YOU DON'T WANT A TATTOO, KID! BY THE TIME I WAS YOUR AGE, I ALREADY HAD THREE!
MAY DU

OH, YEAH? LET'S SEE, DAD!
YOU GOT IT, BUDDY!

HEY... YOU'VE GOT **MOM'S** NAME ON YOU!
HUH? I DO?

SO YOU **DID** CARE ABOUT HER!
WHICH ONE? LULU? CANDI? TOO-TALL?

THAT DOES IT. IF YOU CAN GET A TATTOO WITH MOM'S NAME, SO CAN I!

I WONDER WHICH ONE IT IS...
MISTER? I WANT THAT SMALL "MOM" DESIGN!

HMM... IT COULDN'T BE SUZI— WRONG ERA...
YOU GOT IT, KID! NUMBER 27, "MOM" WITH HEART!

HEY, SON— IS YOUR MOM'S NAME "BOOMER"?
YOU WANT THE SWAS-TIKA?
NO, SHE'S NOT VERY POLITICAL.

HONEY? WE'RE ON OUR WAY HOME! GET DIN-NER STARTED!

HOW WAS YOUR OUT-ING, SIR?
BIG SUCCESS...

THE KID'S OKAY. HE'S TURNING INTO QUITE THE LITTLE MAN!

DAD, WHICH ONE IS THE STOP PEDAL?
EXPERIMENT. I WON'T AL-WAYS BE AROUND TO SHOW YOU.

HOW'S HE DOING, BOOPSIE?
MOSTLY OKAY. HE HAD ANOTHER ROUGH NIGHT.
LLS

YOU KNOW, I WONDER WHETHER THIS THING MIGHT NOT BE STRESS-RELATED.
WELL, B.D. WOULDN'T BE THE FIRST GUY I'VE KNOWN WITH BATTLE FATIGUE!
LLS

NO?
ALEXANDER THE GREAT ONCE TOLD ME THAT FOR YEARS AFTER THE BATTLE OF ISSUS, HE USED TO HAVE TERRIBLE NIGHTMARES.
©B Trudeau

DAMN, YOU'RE CRAZY, GIRL!
I KNOW. ALEX USED TO TEASE ME ABOUT IT.
LLS

THEY COULDN'T NAIL IT DOWN AT THE V.A., RAY. I GOT SOMETHING, BUT NOBODY'S TELLING ME WHAT IT IS!
BU

YOU KNOW, IT COULD BE POST-TRAUMATIC STUFF, MAN. YOU DID HEAVY TIME IN THE GULF. EVER HAVE FLASHBACKS?
BU

SURE. ALL THE TIME. ALMOST EVERY NIGHT.
THERE YOU GO. WHAT'S THE SCENE?

I'M LAYING DOWN FIRE IN A RICE PADDY...
HMM... WRONG WAR. WELL, THAT RULES THAT OUT.
©B Trudeau

THANKS FOR DROPPING BY, RAY.
YOU BE GETTIN' BETTER SOON, B.D., MY BRO.

...AND DON'T WORRY ABOUT YOUR JOB. I TALKED TO THE COMMANDER, AND HE'S COOL WITH YOUR BEING ON LEAVE.
BULLS

THANKS, RAY... HEY, BEFORE YOU GO, MIND IF I ASK YOU A PERSONAL QUESTION?
WHAT'S UP, MAN?
©B Trudeau

DID YOU FALL ASLEEP DURING YOUR LAST HAIRCUT?
YO, I WOULDN'T BE DISSIN' ANYONE'S HEAD, MAN!

RAY THINKS IT MIGHT JUST BE STRESS...
B.D., WHAT DO YOU MEAN "JUST" STRESS? POST-TRAUMATIC STRESS CAN DO LOTS OF DAMAGE TO THE BODY!

YEAH, BUT IT DOESN'T EXPLAIN WHY THIS THING IS SHOWING UP IN FAMILY MEMBERS, TOO! I'M TERRIFIED I MIGHT END UP PASSING IT ON TO YOU!

HEY, DON'T WORRY ABOUT ME, B.D. — IF I COULD SURVIVE SMALL POX AND CONSUMPTION, I CAN DEAL WITH THIS.

BOOPSIE, WHEN DID YOU...
IN 1353 AND 1810, RESPECTIVELY.

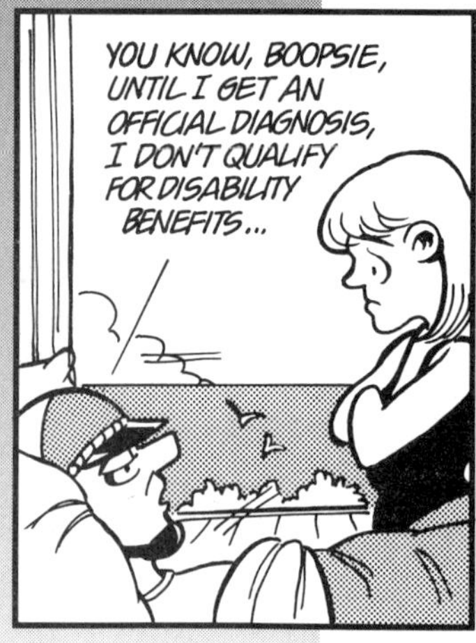
YOU KNOW, BOOPSIE, UNTIL I GET AN OFFICIAL DIAGNOSIS, I DON'T QUALIFY FOR DISABILITY BENEFITS...

AND EVEN IF I DO EVENTUALLY GET THEM, IT'S NOT GOING TO BE ENOUGH TO SUPPORT THIS FAMILY.
NOW, B.D., DON'T BE FRETTING OVER THAT...

I KNOW WE HAVE A LOT OF EXPENSES AND ALL, BUT RIGHT NOW, I'M AT THE PEAK OF MY EARNINGS POTENTIAL!

AS A STARLET?
NO, NO, AS AN O.J. ALTERNATE!

YOU CAN'T IMAGINE WHAT THIS DISEASE IS LIKE, BOOPSIE — JUST LYING HERE, WAITING FOR THE NEXT SYMPTOM CLUSTER...

ACTUALLY, I CAN, B.D. — IT'S SCARY BEING SERIOUSLY ILL. I KNOW – I'VE DIED FROM TYPHUS, DIPHTHERIA, SMALL-POX, T.B., PLAGUE, LEPROSY, TWICE FROM YELLOW FEVER...

WORST OF ALL, I ONCE GOT... GOT...

I'M SORRY... YOU'RE SICK AND I'M BEING COMPETITIVE.
ALWAYS WITH THE CREDITS. IT'S THIS DAMN TOWN.

WHAT YOU HAVE TO REMEMBER IS THAT IN THOSE DAYS, HOLLYWOOD HAD FAMILY VALUES COMING OUT THE WAZOO...

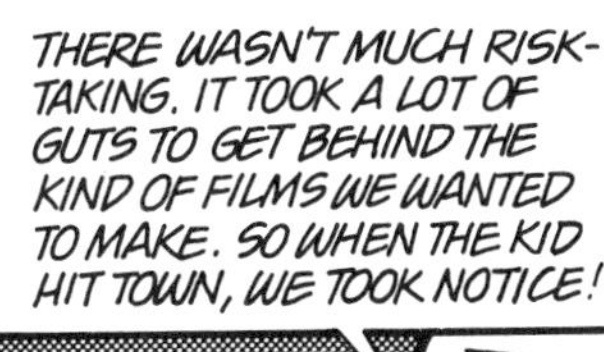
THERE WASN'T MUCH RISK-TAKING. IT TOOK A LOT OF GUTS TO GET BEHIND THE KIND OF FILMS WE WANTED TO MAKE. SO WHEN THE KID HIT TOWN, WE TOOK NOTICE!

HERE, FINALLY, WAS SOMEONE WILLING TO PUT HIS MONEY WHERE HIS MOUTH WAS. THE GUY WAS FOR REAL!
©B Trudeau

SO PHIL GRAMM WAS A PLAYER?
IN THE SEX-SPOOF WORLD? HE **RULED!**

SO THE SENATOR INVESTED IN SEX SPOOFS?
YES. THE ONE THAT GOT MADE WAS "WHITE HOUSE MADNESS"...

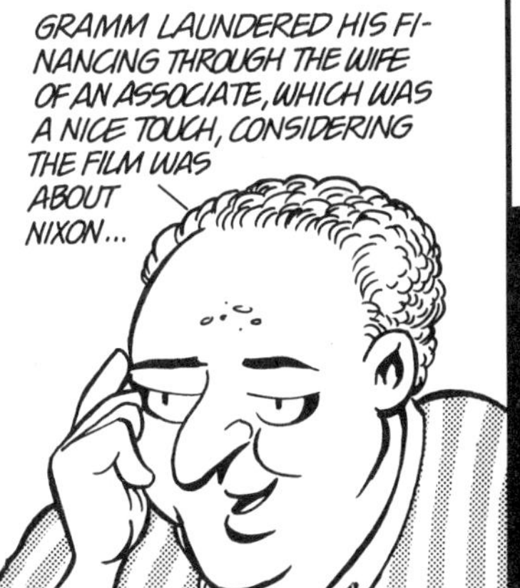
GRAMM LAUNDERED HIS FINANCING THROUGH THE WIFE OF AN ASSOCIATE, WHICH WAS A NICE TOUCH, CONSIDERING THE FILM WAS ABOUT NIXON...

WE THOUGHT HE'D BE HANDS-OFF CREATIVELY, BUT HE WAS ALWAYS SECOND-GUESSING US ON HOW TO STAGE THE SPOOF SCENES.

SO THERE WERE ARTISTIC DIFFERENCES?
HEY, YOU GET INTO BED WITH SOMEONE, IT HAPPENS.
©B Trudeau

SID, WHY DID PHIL GRAMM GET INTO THE FILM BUSINESS?
WELL, I THINK HE HAD THE BUG...

ALSO, HE JUST LOVED SATIRE. HE FIRST GOT INTERESTED IN US WHEN HE SAW "TRUCK STOP WOMEN," OUR SPOOF POKING FUN AT INTERSTATE COMMERCE.
WHEN WE FINALLY GOT DOWN TO MAKING "WHITE HOUSE MADNESS," HE CALLED ME UP AND SAID, "IT'S GOT TO BE A SPOOF. I'M COMMITTED TO MAKING SPOOFS!"
©B Trudeau

SO THE FINAL PRODUCT?
TWO HOURS OF NON-STOP SPOOFING.

YOU SEE, YOU HAVE TO PUT "WHITE HOUSE MADNESS" IN POLITICAL CONTEXT...

GRAMM HAD BEEN A NIXON DEMOCRAT. HE FELT BETRAYED BY WATERGATE. WITH THIS SPOOF HE WAS GETTING BACK AT NIXON.

AND HE WAS DETERMINED TO GET IT RIGHT. AS A YOUNG PRODUCTION ASSISTANT, I TOOK A **LOT** OF CALLS FROM HIM. HE WAS **OBSESSED** WITH THE DETAILS!

PHIL THINKS TRICIA SHOULD WEAR A PINK DEMI-CUP.
TELL HIM TO STICK IT! THIS IS **MY** VISION!

THANKS FOR TALKING TO US, SID...
NOT AT ALL. WHEN DO YOU AIR?

TONIGHT. YOU DON'T HAVE A COPY OF "WHITE HOUSE MADNESS," DO YOU? WE'LL NEED A CLIP...
NO, I LOST MY COPY IN A MUD SLIDE.

KNOW WHERE WE CAN FIND ONE?
HMM... NOT REALLY. YOUR BEST BET IS THE PERSONAL LIBRARY OF SOME SPOOF COLLECTOR...

WELL, IF YOU THINK OF ANY...
TRY THE CLARENCE THOMAS COLLECTION! HIS CURATOR'S AN OLD PAL OF MINE!

MY ... LOOK AT THE **BUILD** ON THIS LITTLE FELLAH!
HA! HA! HA! HA! HA!

SERIOUSLY, I JUST WANT TO SAY I WOULDN'T BE UP HERE IF IT WEREN'T FOR THE ANGEL BEHIND "WHITE HOUSE MADNESS"...

...THE KING OF SEX SPOOFS— MR. **PHIL GRAMM!**
THANK YOU, CHERRIE! I'D JUST LIKE TO THANK THE ACADEMY...
WHAT'S THAT, DEAR?

J.J.? WHERE ARE YOU?
HERE IN ASPEN! I'VE GOT A GROUP SHOW OPENING TONIGHT!

REALLY? HOW EXCITING!
CAN YOU MAKE IT? I HAVEN'T SEEN YOU IN AGES!
Nothin' but Orphans

GOSH, I CAN'T, J.J.— I'M HIP-DEEP IN ORPHANS.
ARE YOU SURE? THERE ARE ALWAYS MUCHO ELIGIBLE MALE BABES AT THESE THINGS.

SIR, ARE YOU IN ANY SHAPE TO COVER?
COVER WHAT?

CONGRATS, J.J.— THE SHOW LOOKS WONDERFUL!
WELL, I'VE ONLY GOT ONE PIECE...

...BUT ASPEN IS A VERY KEY MARKET TO BE SHOWN IN! THE WHOLE ASPEN CRITICAL ESTABLISHMENT WILL BE HERE TONIGHT!

SPEAKING OF WHICH, WOULD THAT BE A TALL, AVAILABLE ART CRITIC RIGHT THERE?
NO, THAT WOULD BE A DELIVERY BOY.

WHATEVER. CATCH YOU LATER.
ENJOY THE SHOW, GIRLFRIEND.

HI, STRANGER!
ZEKE? UH... HI... WHAT ARE YOU...

I HEARD YOU WERE IN TOWN. THOUGHT I'D DROP BY. YOU LOOK GOOD, MAN.
OH...THANKS. YOU TOO, ZEKE. GOSH, IT'S BEEN SO LONG...

HEY, J.J.— WHO'S THIS?
HONEY, YOU REMEMBER ZEKE, DON'T YOU? ZEKE BRENNER?

WELL, SURE! YOU'RE J.J.'S OLD...
I STILL CALL OUT YOUR NAME AT NIGHT, MAN...
WHAT A TREAT FOR YOUR WIFE.

SO HOW'S YOUR OLD LADY, ZEKE?
WE SPLIT UP. LAST YEAR. I'M STILL KIND OF ON THE MEND.

AT THIS POINT, I'M JUST LOOKING FOR SOME-ONE TO HIT THE ROAD WITH— A FRIEND, WHO LOVES DINERS AND JUKEBOXES AND DESERT SUNSETS AND DRINKING CHAMPAGNE FROM A PAPER CUP...

©B'Trudeau

ZEKE... I...
WELL, OKAY, BUT I'VE GOT TO GO HOME AND GET MY PURSE.

ZEKE, WANT TO GO GET SOME COF-FEE? GET CAUGHT UP?
I THOUGHT YOU'D NEVER ASK, MAN...
WHAT?

HOW MORTIFYING! I THOUGHT YOU WERE COMING ON TO ME, SIR! TALK ABOUT CROSSED SIGNALS!

I GUESS I JUST JUMPED TO CONCLUSIONS BECAUSE I'M SO...SO... WELL, YOU DON'T WANT TO KNOW...
©B'Trudeau

YEAH, PROBABLY NOT.
MAN-HUNGRY! I'M SO MAN-HUNGRY! THERE! I'VE SAID IT!

HAVE YOU SEEN CLINT EASTWOOD'S NEW MOVIE, J.J.? THAT BRIDGES THING?
NOT YET...

WELL, CLINT'S CHAR-ACTER IS ME! I AM THAT TOUGH BUT SOULFUL NEW-AGE COWBOY!

...AND YOU— YOU'RE MY ONE TRUE LOVE, A STAR CREATURE, TREMBLING WITH LONGING!
BUT ZEKE— I'M...I'M MARRIED.
©B'Trudeau

EXACTLY! JUST LIKE IN THE MOVIE!
WHOA... THAT'S TOO WEIRD...

C'MON, MAN, YOU GOTTA ADMIT IT—WE'RE VERY MUCH IN A POTENTIAL "BRIDGES OF MADISON COUNTY" SCENARIO HERE...

HEY, MAN, YOU **SURE** YOU HAVEN'T SEEN THE MOVIE YET?
I DON'T KNOW, ZEKE, I...

YOU PLAY WITH YOUR HAIR THE SAME WAY MERYL STREEP DOES. THERE'S THE SAME SUBTLE SENSUALITY!
OF COURSE I'M SURE. WHY?

THERE IS? REALLY?
IT'S A SIGN, MAN!

ZEKE, I DON'T KNOW ABOUT USING A MOVIE AS A MODEL FOR MY LIFE...
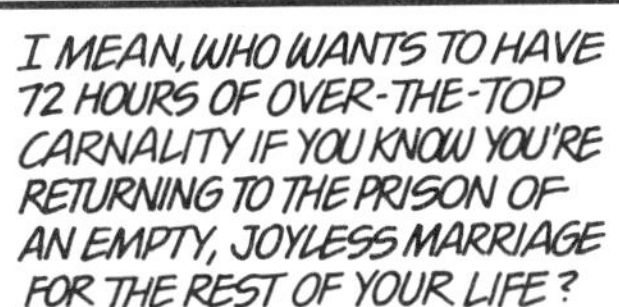
I MEAN, WHO WANTS TO HAVE 72 HOURS OF OVER-THE-TOP CARNALITY IF YOU KNOW YOU'RE RETURNING TO THE PRISON OF AN EMPTY, JOYLESS MARRIAGE FOR THE REST OF YOUR LIFE?

WHOA... SLOW DOWN, MAN. YOU GOTTA TAKE IT ONE STEP AT A TIME.
WHAT DO YOU MEAN?

WELL, LIKE THAT CARNAL THING. WE COULD **BUILD** TO THAT.
LEAVING WHAT—68 HOURS? PASS.

WHAT ARE WE REALLY TALKING ABOUT HERE, ZEKE? ARE WE TALKING ABOUT ME TRASHING MY LIFE FOR A FEW DAYS OF EMPTY PASSION?...
NO, NOT AT ALL.

IT'S NOT ABOUT THAT, MAN. IT'S ABOUT PICKING FLOWERS. IT'S ABOUT MAKING SALADS, QUOTING YEATS, SLOW DANCING IN THE MOONLIGHT. IT'S ABOUT... LOVE.

ZEKE, HOW MANY TIMES DID YOU SEE THIS MOVIE?
THREE. I'M TRYING TO IMPROVE MYSELF, MAN.

ZEKE, IF I RUN OFF WITH YOU, I'LL PAY A **VERY** BIG PRICE. I HAVE TO BE SURE...
I UNDERSTAND, MAN. I UNDERSTAND A LOT OF THINGS I DIDN'T USED TO.

IT CAN'T JUST BE ABOUT GETTING NASTY IN SOME CHEAP MOTEL. I WANT TO BE WOOED...
WOOED? YOU GOT IT, MAN!

I'M OLDER AND WISER NOW—LIKE ROBERT KINCAID! I'M GOING TO WOO YOUR **SOCKS** OFF! I'M GOING TO TAKE YOUR **BREATH** AWAY! ARE YOU READY, MAN?
©B Trudeau

OH, YES... **YES!** I'M **READY!**
BAD NEWS, GUYS. ALL THE MEN WERE TAKEN.

J.J., I THINK I SEE WHAT'S GOING ON HERE, AND I BEG YOU TO RECONSIDER...
HONEY, HOW MANY SHOTS AT REAL HAPPINESS DO WE GET?

IN MY CASE, NOT TOO MANY. BUT YOU AND MIKE...
LOOK AT ZEKE—WHAT DO YOU SEE? UNTAMED, MYSTERIOUS, CHARISMATIC! NOW THINK OF MIKE. WHAT COMES TO MIND?

GIVE ME A MINUTE...
HONEY, I DON'T **HAVE** A MINUTE! WE'RE TALKING ABOUT WHAT'S LEFT OF MY **LIFE!**
©B Trudeau

SO HOW'D YOUR OLD MAN TAKE THE NEWS, J.J.?

UM... I HAVEN'T TOLD HIM YET...
WHAT?...
©B Trudeau

YOU DIDN'T CALL HIM BEFORE WE LEFT?
NO... I LOST MY NERVE.

STILL NO ANSWER! MOMMY MUST HAVE RUN AWAY WITH A COWBOY!
WOW... A **REAL** COWBOY?

HELLO?
MIKE? I'M LEAVING YOU.

WHAT?...
I'M TIRED OF SETTLING, OF LIVING IN REGRET. I'M FOLLOWING MY BLISS. GOODBYE, MIKE.
J.J.! WAIT...
DADDY! WAKE UP! IT'S MOM ON THE PHONE!

HELLO?
MIKE? I'M LEAVING YOU.

ZEKE? YOU'RE LEAVING ME FOR ZEKE?
HE'S MY SOUL MATE, MIKE. I DIDN'T REALIZE WHAT I HAD.

AND YOU DON'T REALIZE WHAT YOU'RE GIVING UP! J.J., I'VE BEEN THROUGH THIS—I KNOW!

REMEMBER MY LITTLE INFATUATION WITH NICOLE? SHE WANTED ME TO GO AWAY WITH HER, BUT I TOUGHED IT OUT! I STAYED THE COURSE!

SO YOU WERE AN IDIOT.
WELL, OKAY, SURE, IT LOOKS THAT WAY NOW...

WHAT'S SHE SAY, DADDY? WHEN'S MOMMY COMING HOME?

UM... I'M NOT SURE, HONEY. IT SEEMS MOMMY'S FOUND A NEW... A NEW FRIEND.
FRIEND? THAT'S RIDICULOUS! SHE HAS YOU!

...AND YOU'RE THE NICEST, HANDSOMEST, FUNNIEST, SMARTEST, MOST TALENTED MAN IN THE WHOLE WORLD!

WELL, SURE, ON PAPER, HONEY, BUT...
MOMMY'S JOKING WITH YOU, DAD. CALL HER BACK.

I'M SURE SHE'LL BE BACK, HONEY. MOMMY'S JUST GONE A LITTLE BIT CRAZY...
IT'S MY FAULT, ISN'T IT? IT'S SOMETHING I DID.

NO, NO, ALEX, YOU CAN'T THINK THAT! MOMMY LOVES YOU VERY MUCH...

IF IT'S ANYBODY'S FAULT, IT'S MINE. I'VE BEEN A TERRIBLE PROVIDER. MOMMY'S NEW FRIEND IS PROBABLY JUST GIVING HER ALL THE THINGS I HAVEN'T BEEN ABLE TO...

YOU CAN'T EVEN PAY FOR THE ROOM?
I THOUGHT YOU WERE THIS BIG NEW YORK ART STAR, MAN!

NOTHIN' BUT ORPHANS, MS. HUAN SPEAKING.
HONEY, IT'S ME, J.J.! I'M IN A JAM!

WHAT KIND OF JAM, J.J.?
IT TURNS OUT WE'RE BOTH BROKE. COULD YOU WIRE ME $200 TO TIDE US OVER? JUST UNTIL I FIND A JOB...

WELL... SURE, WHY NOT? IF I CAN'T HAVE MY OWN LOVE LIFE, I MIGHT AS WELL UNDERWRITE YOURS.
YOU'RE THE BEST, GIRLFRIEND!

I WANT REPORTS, THOUGH. INCLUDING THE GOOD PARTS.
YOU GOT IT! LAST NIGHT HE CAME TO ME LIKE A PANTHER! NO, A WILDEBEEST!

SIR, HAVE YOU EVER FELT LIKE GIVING UP EVERYTHING FOR THE LOVE OF A WOMAN?
YEAH, ONCE IN NEW YORK...

IT WAS SO LONG AGO, I DON'T REMEMBER HER CLEARLY, BUT IT WAS THE MOST EXTRAORDINARY THREE DAYS OF MY LIFE...

I DO RECALL THE SMELL OF HER HAIR AND THE COLOR OF HER EYES. AND I'LL NEVER FORGET HER LAST WORDS TO ME.

YOU DON'T HAVE TO SHARE THEM WITH ME, SIR, IF IT'S TOO...
"WILL YOU BE PUTTING THIS ON YOUR VISA CARD?"

YOU KNOW, ZEKE, YOUR "BRIDGES" MODEL DOESN'T SEEM TO BE HOLDING UP FOR US. FRANCESCA DIDN'T LEAVE HER FAMILY.

OKAY, HOW ABOUT "ELVIRA MADIGAN," MAN? WE COULD KEY OFF THAT...
NEVER SAW IT. WHAT HAPPENS?

WELL, LIKE US, THEY'RE LOVERS ON THE LAM. THEY RUN OUT OF MONEY, AND THEY'RE FINALLY REDUCED TO EATING GRASS AND BUGS, SO THE GUY BLOWS AWAY BOTH OF THEM.

COOL. DO THEY MAKE THE NEWS?
NO, THIS IS BEFORE NEWS. MOZART DID THE MUSIC.

HEY, MAN, I'M GOING TO STOP IN THIS TOWN UP AHEAD TO GET SOME SMOKES, OKAY?

OKAY. WANT ME TO DO ANYTHING WHILE WE'RE HERE?

NAH, JUST HANG. LEAN AGAINST THE TRUCK, PRESS A COLD DR. PEPPER AGAINST YOUR NECK, AND STOP TRAFFIC UNTIL I GET BACK.

GOD, I HAVEN'T DONE THAT IN AGES.
I'LL GO WATCH FROM THE POOL HALL.

J.J., WHAT **ARE** YOU DOING, GIRLFRIEND?

YOU'RE FEELING GOOD ABOUT BEING A WOMAN, THAT'S WHAT! BEEN AROUND THE TRACK, SURE, BUT YOU STILL FILL OUT YOUR CUT-OFFS, GIRL! **WHEW!**

YOU CAN FEEL 50 PAIRS OF HUNGRY EYES, MEN WHO WANT ME, WHO WOULD GIVE UP **EVERYTHING** THEY HOLD DEAR FOR ME!

CALLING HUGH GRANT.
NAH. THEY MUST BE SHOOTING A COMMERCIAL.

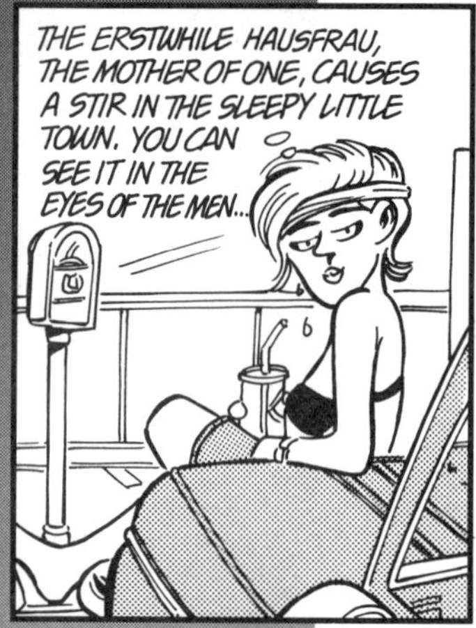
THE ERSTWHILE HAUSFRAU, THE MOTHER OF ONE, CAUSES A STIR IN THE SLEEPY LITTLE TOWN. YOU CAN SEE IT IN THE EYES OF THE MEN...

"WHO IS THIS... THIS GODDESS?" THEY WHISPER. "WHERE DID SHE COME FROM?"
EXCUSE ME, MISS?

YES?
MISS, I'M AFRAID YOUR ACTIVITIES ARE IN VIOLATION OF TOWN ORDINANCES.

HOW'D IT GO?
ROMANCE IS DEAD.
GB Trudeau

ZEKE, I CAN'T **BELIEVE** I MADE SUCH A FOOL OF MYSELF IN THAT TOWN!
HEY, C'MON, YOU WERE JUST HAVIN' FUN! DON'T BEAT YOURSELF UP!

I WAS ACTING LIKE A BIMBO, ZEKE!
YOU WERE NOT. YOU WERE ACTING LIKE SOMEONE **WHO'S BEEN** STARVED FOR ATTENTION!

YOU DON'T **REALLY** WANT TO BE A BABE ANYMORE—YOU'VE DONE THAT! AND I **WAS** WITH YOU! NOW IT'S TIME TO MOVE INTO YOUR POST-BABE PERIOD. AND I'LL BE WITH YOU FOR THAT, TOO!
GB Trudeau

OH, ZEKE, YOU DO SAY THE MOST...
I MEAN, WHO **CARES** ABOUT ARM FLAB, MAN? YOU KNOW?

WHAT TIME WOULD IT BE IN NEW YORK RIGHT NOW, ZEKE?
WELL, LET'S SEE ... IT'D BE ABOUT 9:15...

YOU STILL WORRYING ABOUT YOUR FAMILY, MAN?

A LITTLE. BUT IT'S BEEN NEARLY SIX WEEKS SINCE I SPLIT. I'M SURE MIKE'S STARTING TO GET IT TOGETHER BY NOW...
GB Trudeau

I'M OFF TO DAY CAMP, DAD. DON'T FORGET TO BUY FOOD.
FOOD... OKAY... SEE YA...

Welcome to the Walden University Web site. Please enter your affiliation and class.
CLIK! CLIK!

WALDEN COLLEGE, CLASS OF '83.
Class of '83. Currently in chat room: Mark Slackmeyer...
CLIK! CLIK!

MARK! WHAT ARE YOU DOING UP AT THIS HOUR?
Hi, Mike. I'm looking for love.
CLIK! CLIK!

REALLY? WELL, GOOD LUCK. GOTTA RUN.
You jerk--I don't mean this very second.
TAP! CLIK!

DADDY, WHY ARE YOU STILL UP? WHO ARE YOU TALKING TO NOW?

JUST SOME OF MY BUDDIES FROM COLLEGE, SQUIRT. THIS IS THE WALDEN WEB SITE...

SEE, THAT WINDOW LISTS WHO'S IN THE CHAT ROOM. THERE'S UNCLE MARK... AND BERNIE... YOU REMEMBER BERNIE... AND... AND...

AND...
WHO'S NICOLE?

Mike? It's me, Nicole. How've you been, stranger?
UH-OH...

UM... NEVER BETTER, NICOLE. YOU KNOW, GETTING BY, DOING OKAY. REALLY CAN'T COMPLAIN.
TAP! TAP!

J.J. left you, didn't she?
Mike? Ed Biddle. Did you send in your class dues yet?

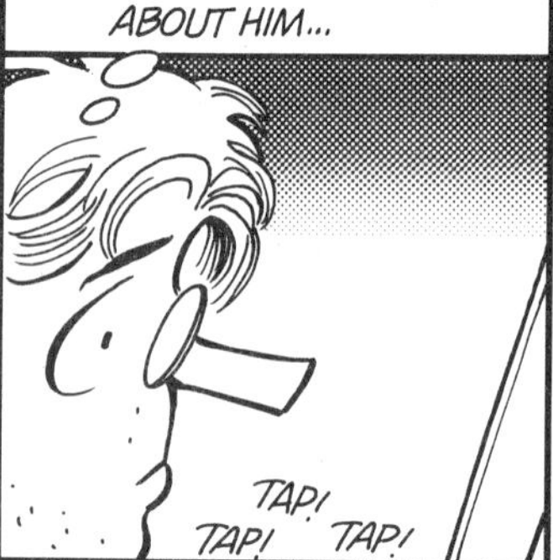

No one here has a clue whether I'm still a babe or whether I've ballooned up again. It forces people to judge me as a person.

HEAR THAT? THE UNEXPECTED KNOCK ON THE DOOR? IT CAN ONLY MEAN ONE THING—THE ONSET OF MIKE'S SUMMER DAYDREAM!
KNOCK! KNOCK!

KNOCK! KNOCK!
AND JUST IN TIME FROM THE LOOKS OF THINGS! COULD THIS BOY USE A BREAK FROM REALITY OR WHAT?

MIKE! DON'T KEEP YOUR MYSTERIOUS CALLER WAITING! HE'S HERE TO CHANGE YOUR LIFE!
RIGHT. AND THEN BREAK MY HEART WHEN I SNAP OUT OF IT. PASS.

KNOCK! KNOCK!
UM... COULD I HAVE YOUR DAYDREAM, THEN?
HELP YOURSELF. UNLESS IT'S A BABE.

MIKE'S ANNUAL SUMMER DAYDREAM IS UNDER WAY.
HI, DUDE!
BERNIE! YOU'RE THE MYSTERIOUS CALLER?

MICHAEL! JUST THE MAN I WAS LOOKING FOR!
MIKE, NO OFFENSE, BUT ANY DAYDREAM FEATURING BERNIE IS GONNA BE A SNOOZE...

I'D LIKE YOU TO HEAD UP MARKETING AT MY NEW SOFTWARE COMPANY—MOVE TO SEATTLE, TELECOMMUTE FROM YOUR HOME OVERLOOKING PUGET SOUND, WEAR FLANNEL SHIRTS, THE WHOLE NINE YARDS!

BOR-ING! DIDN'T I TELL YOU?
YOU'RE GOING TO START ME AT 300 G'S, AREN'T YOU? I CAN TELL!

IN MIKE'S SUMMERTIME FANTASY, OLD LABMATE BERNIE OFFERS HIM A DREAM JOB...
MIKE, I WANT YOU TO COME TO WORK AT MY NEW SOFTWARE COMPANY...

THE FINANCIAL PACKAGE IS ALL SPELLED OUT IN THIS ROLLING 5-YEAR CONTRACT—INCLUDING THE STOCK OPTIONS AND THE SIGNING BONUS!

GOOD GOD, BERNIE! YOU'RE INVITING ME TO JOIN THE... JOIN THE...
GO AHEAD, SAY IT!

THE UPPER-MIDDLE CLASS!
IT'S WHERE YOU BELONG, BIG GUY!

I DON'T GET IT, BERNIE! WHY ME?
YOU'RE QUALIFIED, AND AFTER YEARS OF UNDEREMPLOYMENT, YOU'RE HUNGRY!

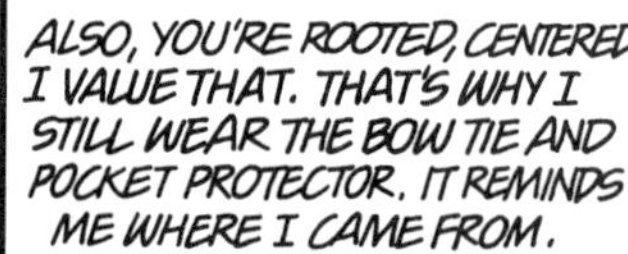
ALSO, YOU'RE ROOTED, CENTERED. I VALUE THAT. THAT'S WHY I STILL WEAR THE BOW TIE AND POCKET PROTECTOR. IT REMINDS ME WHERE I CAME FROM.

EVEN THOUGH I JET AROUND THE COUNTRY SPEAKING TO BUSINESS LEADERS WHO HANG ON MY EVERY WORD, I STILL LOOK LIKE THE SAME AWKWARD, GEEKY MISFIT I WAS IN COLLEGE!

HEY... I WAS LIKE THAT, TOO! REMEMBER?
REMEMBER? HELL, MIKE, EVEN I SHUNNED YOU!

MIKE ADJUSTS QUICKLY TO HIS NEW LIFE IN SEATTLE...
TRY THAT NEW COFFEE I SENT OVER?
IT WAS THE BEST!

...AS DOES DAUGHTER ALEX.
BYE, DAD! I'M OFF FOR THE EXCELLENT PUBLIC SCHOOL JUST DOWN THE STREET!
BYE, BABE! I WON'T WORRY BECAUSE THE NEIGHBORHOOD'S SO SAFE!

HIS WORK IS REWARDING...
GREAT RELEASE STRATEGY, GANG! LET'S GO WITH IT!

...INSANELY SO.
I'M HAVING TOO MUCH FUN. I'VE COME TO GIVE THE MONEY BACK.
NO CAN DO, MIKE. IF I LET YOU, EVERYONE WILL WANT TO!

WHAT A GREAT SUMMER DAYDREAM! I WISH IT DIDN'T HAVE TO END...
IT DOESN'T!

WHAT?
GREAT NEWS, BRO! THERE WAS SOME SORT OF PROGRAMMING MIX-UP...

TURNS OUT ALL THIS ISN'T THE PRODUCT OF YOUR FEVERISH IMAGINATION — IT'S AN ACTUAL STORY LINE!

YOU MEAN, THIS IS REALLY HAPPENING?
WELL, WITHIN THE BOUNDS OF FICTION.

LET ME GET THIS STRAIGHT, ZONK— MY DAYDREAM IS **ACTUALLY** HAPPENING TO ME?
THAT'S RIGHT...

OF COURSE, IT'S BEEN ADJUSTED FOR REALITY. THIS HOUSE IS JUST A RENTAL, YOUR HEALTH INSURANCE ISN'T COMPREHENSIVE, AND YOU DON'T REALLY HAVE STOCK OPTIONS.

AH, SO WHAT? THE REST OF MY NEW LIFE IS **MAGNIFICENT**! THE CLEAN AIR, THE SAFE ENVIRONMENT, THE SPECTACULAR VIEW, AND... AND...

WHERE'S MY LEXUS?
HEY, WITH A VIEW LIKE THIS, WHO NEEDS TO GO ANYWHERE?

ZONKER, ARE YOU **SURE** MY NEW LIFE ISN'T JUST A FANTASY?
POSITIVE! I DOUBLE-CHECKED THE WORK ORDER PERSONALLY...

THERE ARE A FEW THINGS THAT NEED YOUR SIGNATURE, THOUGH. WAIVERS, INDEMNIFICATIONS, LICENSING RIGHTS, THAT SORT OF THING...

ALSO, CHANGE-OF-ADDRESS CARDS, CREDIT CARD NOTIFICATIONS AND BANK AUTHORIZATIONS TO TRANSFER ASSETS FROM YOUR FANTASY BACK TO REAL LIFE.

I DON'T RECALL MY FANTASY HAVING ANY PAPERWORK.
OF COURSE NOT—THAT'S WHAT MADE IT A FANTASY.

BERNIE? GOT A MINUTE?
MIKE! I WAS HOPING YOU'D DROP BY!

YOU WERE?
YEAH, I HEARD THE GOOD NEWS!
WHAT GOOD NEWS?
THAT THIS STORY LINE ISN'T A FANTASY! THAT IT'S **ACTUALLY** HAPPENING TO YOU! CONGRATULATIONS!

UM... THANKS. YOU'RE COOL WITH THIS?
100%! OF COURSE, WE'LL HAVE TO SWITCH YOU OVER TO A REAL WORLD SALARY...

BERNIE, I'VE GOT TO KNOW SOMETHING...
SURE– WHAT IS IT, MIKE?

WHEN I TOOK THE JOB HERE, I WAS JUST FREE-ASSOCIATING, PIGGY-BACKING ON YOUR REAL WORLD SUCCESS...
REALLY? I DIDN'T KNOW THAT.

YOU **DIDN'T?** YOU MEAN I **WASN'T** GIVEN PREFERENTIAL CONSIDERATION?
MIKE! I'M OFFENDED!

WHAT A RELIEF! SEE, I'M A REPUBLICAN NOW, AND...
RELAX– YOU WERE CLEARLY THE BEST FORMER COLLEGE ROOMMATE FOR THE JOB!

POPSTER?

HI, ALEX! HOW'D SCHOOL GO?
DAD, ARE YOU SURE OUR NEW LIFE IS JUST A DAYDREAM?

ACTUALLY, IT TURNS OUT IT'S NOT, SWEETHEART—IT'S ALL **ACTUALLY** HAPPENING TO US! IT'S **REAL LIFE!**
REAL LIFE?

PRETTY EXCITING, HUH?
WELL, THAT EXPLAINS THE STABBING.

DAD, IF OUR NEW LIFE IS HERE IN SEATTLE, HOW WILL MOMMY FIND US?
WELL, I'VE LEFT A FORWARDING ADDRESS...

...BUT I DON'T THINK MOMMY REALLY **WANTS** TO FIND US YET, BABE.

YOU SEE, YOU AND I ARE BACK IN THE REAL WORLD. BUT MOMMY'S NOT READY YET—SHE NEEDS MORE TIME.

OKAY, HOW'S THIS? "I'D LIKE TO THANK THE ACADEMY FOR..."
NO, NO. BLOW 'EM OFF! THE TOWN NEVER GAVE YOU A **THING!**

GOOD EVENING. TODAY THE ASSAULT ON FEDERAL SAFETY AND ENVIRONMENTAL REGULATIONS CONTINUED UNABATED...

ON THE SENATE FLOOR, DEMOCRATS FOUGHT A LOSING BATTLE AGAINST A MAJORITY COMMITTED TO THE WHOLESALE DISMANTLING OF PUBLIC SAFETY STANDARDS...

...WHILE IN THE CAUCUS ROOM, SENATOR BOB DOLE MET WITH THE BUSINESS LOBBY COMMUNITY TO SOLICIT THEIR "INPUT"...

OKAY, WHO'D LIKE TO REWRITE THE CLEAN AIR ACT?
RIGHT HERE, SENATOR!
I'LL TAKE A SHOT!
ME!
ME!

SENATOR DOLE INVITES INDUSTRY TO REWRITE ITS OWN REGULATIONS...
WHAT WE'RE DOING TODAY, OF COURSE, IS NOT WITHOUT POLITICAL RISK...

AFTER ALL, WE'RE ATTEMPTING TO GUT SAFETY AND ENVIRONMENTAL LAWS WITH PROVEN EFFECTIVENESS AND POPULARITY, LAWS THAT ACTUALLY WORKED...

BUT AT A TRAGIC COST TO OUR STOCKHOLDERS!
BAM!

I WAS GETTING TO THAT, JIM.
OH... SORRY, SENATOR... I'M A LITTLE DISORIENTED HERE.

LET ME JUST SAY AGAIN IT'S A PLEASURE TO BE WORKING ON REGULATORY REFORM WITH THE LOBBYIST COMMUNITY! IT'S A GREAT DAY FOR COST-BENEFIT ANALYSIS!

OKAY, LET'S TRY TO GET A CONSENSUS ON SOME FUNDAMENTALS. FIRST OF ALL, WHAT'S AN AMERICAN LIFE WORTH?

MEAT INDUSTRY?
SENATOR DOLE, WE PUT THAT FIGURE AT ABOUT $35.

REALLY? WE GOT IT PEGGED AT 12¢...
THAT'S WHAT I MEANT.

WHAT WE WANT TO DO, THEN, IS REQUIRE REGULATORY AGENCIES TO DO COST-BENEFIT ANALYSIS OF EVEN THEIR MOST EFFECTIVE RULES...

...AND NATURALLY, WE SEEK YOUR INPUT HERE.
ONE SUGGESTION, SENATOR...

IF YOU MAKE THE COST-BENEFIT REQUIREMENTS ONEROUS ENOUGH, THE AGENCIES WILL BE SO TIED UP TRYING TO DEFEND THEIR REGULATIONS, THEY'LL HAVE NO RESOURCES FOR **ENFORCING** THEM!
ACTUALLY, WE ALREADY THOUGHT OF THAT, PHIL.
EXCELLENT! CAN WE PROVIDE THE LANGUAGE?

BOB, LET ME SEE IF I UNDERSTAND YOUR REGULATORY REFORM DRAFT...

SAY, JUST SAY, I'M POLLUTING. WHAT IF THE FEDS DO ONE OF THESE COST-BENEFIT ANALYSES, AND I **STILL** HAVE TO CLEAN UP?

IN THAT CASE, YOU GO TO COURT! WE'VE MADE IT **MUCH** EASIER TO SUE THE GOVERNMENT!
AND WE'RE ALLOWED TO **CONTINUE** POLLUTING WHILE IT'S TIED UP IN COURT?

I'M TELLING YOU, JIM— THIS IS **REAL** REFORM!
WHEW. I GUESS! IT'S JUST HARD TO BELIEVE!

SENATOR DOLE, DO YOU THINK YOUR GUTTING OF THE HEALTH AND SAFETY LAWS WILL PLAY WELL IN THE UPCOMING PRESIDENTIAL RACE?

YES. I THINK THE AMERICAN PEOPLE FULLY SUPPORT REGULATORY RELIEF FOR INDUSTRY. THEY UNDERSTAND THAT BUSINESSES NEED TO BE HEALTHY, TOO.

I CERTAINLY DON'T THINK IT'S AN ISSUE THAT WILL COME BACK TO HAUNT ME, IF THAT'S WHAT YOU MEAN.

LATER...
LADIES AND GENTLEMEN, I GIVE YOU SENATOR BOB "E. COLI" **DOLE**!

HEY, MEN-WHAT'S UP?
WE'RE LOADING IN THE NEW WINDOWS 95 OPERATING SYSTEM, MIKE.

OH, YEAH? HOW'S IT LOOK?
DON'T KNOW YET. I'M STILL TRYING TO CLEAR ENOUGH MEMORY FOR IT...

Attention User: You call this capacity? Reboot when you're ready to play.

SON OF A... IT'S DISSING MY HARD DRIVE!
BACK OFF, HANK. DON'T MAKE IT LOSE FACE...

WHAT'S WRONG? WHY'S THE NEW WINDOWS BALKING?
IT'S GREEDY. IT'S HOLDING OUT FOR 16 MEGABYTES RAM...

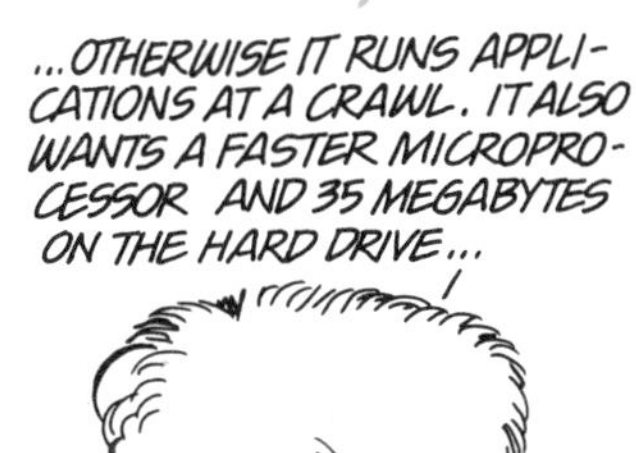
...OTHERWISE IT RUNS APPLICATIONS AT A CRAWL. IT ALSO WANTS A FASTER MICROPROCESSOR AND 35 MEGABYTES ON THE HARD DRIVE...

...WITH 89 MORE FOR OFFICE PROGRAMS, AND... HEY... IT JUST TURNED ON THE PRINTER!

IT'S A COMPLETE LIST OF ITS DEMANDS!
GIVE NO QUARTER! HOLD IT TO ITS BOX SPECS!

HEY, HANK, DID YOU GET WINDOWS 95 LOADED IN YET?
YUP. TAKE A LOOK...

ICONS JUST LIKE APPLE'S, FILES AND FOLDERS JUST LIKE APPLE'S, TASK BARS, MENUS, TRASH FUNCTIONS—THE WHOLE APPLE DESKTOP ENVIRONMENT!

MAN... THEY CAN GET AWAY WITH THAT?
CHECK THE BACK OF THE BOX.

"THIS PRODUCT SUPPORTED BY 3,000 LAWYERS."
THAT'S ONE HELLUVA PLATFORM.

BERNIE, I DON'T GET IT—WHY ARE WE GOING WITH MICROSOFT IF WINDOWS 95 IS JUST ANOTHER APPLE RIP-OFF?
MIKE, WHO MAKES THE SOFTWARE THAT RUNS 80% OF THE WORLD'S P.C.'S?

MICROSOFT, OF COURSE.
AND DOES THE WORLD RUN ON COMPUTERS?

SURE.
SO WHO RULES THE WORLD?

SIGH ...WHY DON'T WE JUST GIVE BILL GATES ALL THE MONEY NOW AND GET IT OVER WITH?
PRIDE.

THE THING IS, MIKE, IT DOESN'T REALLY MATTER WHAT YOU OR I THINK OF WINDOWS. WE DEVELOP SOFTWARE, AND WINDOWS RULES!

YOU GOTTA DISCOUNT ANY NEGATIVE BUZZ YOU HEAR. A LOT OF IT'S JEALOUSY. WHO WOULDN'T WANT TO BE SITTING WHERE GATES IS?

I MYSELF WOULD LOVE TO HAVE A STRANGLEHOLD ON A WHOLE INDUSTRY. I'VE OFTEN FANTASIZED ABOUT GETTING THAT FIRST PHONE CALL FROM THE JUSTICE DEPARTMENT!

YOU HAVE?
ABSOLUTELY. THAT'S WHEN YOU'VE ARRIVED!

HI, BABE!
DADSTER! SOMEONE DOWNLOADED A NEW SYSTEM INTO OUR COMPUTER TODAY!

THAT WOULD BE WINDOWS 95...
RIGHT. IT'S NOT BAD. IT'S GOT A COOL NEW GAME ON IT...

ONLY PROBLEM I NOTICED WAS THE P.C. SOMETIMES SLOWED DOWN WHEN I ASKED IT TO DO TWO THINGS AT ONCE...

THAT'S CALLED MULTI-TASKING, SQUIRT. YOU SEE...
OH, RIGHT. ANYWAY, I REWROTE THE CODE. IT'S OKAY NOW.

GOOD MORNING, MR. PRESIDENT!

HEY... WHAT ARE YOU DOING HERE?
I CAME TO COMMENT, SIR!

WHEN I HEARD THERE WAS A 90-DAY PERIOD OF PUBLIC COMMENT ON YOUR TEEN-AGE SMOKING RESTRICTIONS, I RUSHED OVER PRONTO!

UM... WILL THIS TAKE LONG?
NO, I CAN ONLY STAY A MONTH.
WHERE DO I FRESH-EN UP?
©BTrudeau

MR. PRESIDENT, I KNOW HOW VALUABLE YOUR TIME IS...
IN FACT, I WOULDN'T BE HERE IF IT WEREN'T FOR YOUR FORMIDABLE REPUTATION!

WHAT REPU-TATION IS THAT?
YOU KNOW— FOR BEING... REASONABLE!

YOU MEAN, FOR EQUIV-OCATING?
IF THAT'S WHAT IT TAKES! YOU'RE KNOWN AND RE-SPECTED FOR IT!

OH, YEAH? WHERE?
VIRGINIA FARM COUNTRY! YOU'RE LIKE A GOD THERE!
©BTrudeau

LET'S GET DOWN TO IT, SHALL WE, SIR?
THESE ANTI-SMOKING CURBS ARE JUST POLI-TICS, AREN'T THEY?
POLI-TICS?

SURE! TOBACCO'S A SOUTHERN ISSUE, BUT YOU'VE ALREADY WRITTEN OFF THE SOUTH IN '96! SO YOU SHORE UP YOUR SUPPORT IN THE OTHER STATES BY LOOKING BOLD AND PRESIDENTIAL!

HEY, YOU'RE RIGHT—THERE IS A POLITICAL UPSIDE! I DIDN'T THINK OF THAT!
YOU DIDN'T?

NOPE! AND TO THINK I WAS GET-TING READY TO CAVE...
DOH!
STUPID! STUPID!
©BTrudeau

SIR, THESE ANTI-SMOKING MEASURES ARE A TROJAN HORSE! THEY CONCEAL A HIDDEN AGENDA—A FUTURE BAN ON ALL SMOKING!

MR. BUTTS, I ONLY HEAR YOU ATTACKING WHAT WE MIGHT DO. MAKE THE CASE AGAINST WHAT WE'VE ACTUALLY DONE.

THE CASE AGAINST RESTRICTING TEEN SMOKING? WITH ALL DUE RESPECT, SIR, THAT'S A NO-BRAINER! PIECE OF CAKE! NO SWEAT! SIMPLE AS PIE!
OH, REALLY?
HECK, YES! CAKE WALK! DONE DEAL. NO PROBLEMO! GOT IT COVERED!

MR. PRESIDENT, I THINK I'VE GOT AN ARGUMENT HERE YOU'LL FIND IRRESISTIBLE!

MOOLA! MUCHO MOOLA! AND THERE'S LOTS MORE WHERE THIS COMES FROM! AND I DO MEAN LOTS!

HUH? HUH?

LEON? GET ME THE F.B.I.
HOW ODD... THAT ALWAYS WORKS WITH CONGRESS.

HMM... THE PREZ IS PROVING TOUGHER THAN I THOUGHT...
BETTER TRY A MORE EMOTIONAL APPROACH!
ARE YOU STILL HERE?

MR. PRESIDENT, YOU HAVE TO UNDERSTAND...

IF YOU BAN ADS AND PROMOTIONS FOR TEENS, IT'LL MEAN THE END OF... SOB!... OF...
OF WHAT?

...CUTE CARTOON CHARACTERS!
WAAH!
I FEEL YOUR PAIN. NOW BEAT IT.

HELLO, I'M JOANIE CAUCUS. FOR THE PAST 32 MONTHS, THE SENATE HAS FAILED TO HOLD PUBLIC HEARINGS ON THE ALLEGED SEXUAL MISCONDUCT OF ONE OF ITS OWN...

TODAY THE "PACKWOOD 19" ARE SEEKING RECOURSE. THEY HAVE ENGAGED ME TO SECURE THIS SPACE FOR THE ENTIRE WEEK SO THAT THEY MAY HOLD THEIR OWN PUBLIC HEARINGS.

BY BEARING WITNESS HERE, THEY HOPE TO FIND A KIND OF JUSTICE THAT HAS BEEN DENIED THEM FOR SO LONG
BY... BY...
R-R-R-R-R-R-R R RR!

EXCUSE ME?
JUST TIDYING UP.
TRY TO LEAVE IT HOW YOU FOUND IT.

THE PACKWOOD 19, UNHEARD FROM—THANKS TO THE SENATE ETHICS COMMITTEE—UNTIL NOW!

THIS SPACE HAS BEEN LEASED THROUGH SATURDAY SO THAT THESE WOMEN CAN FINALLY TELL THEIR STORIES...

THAT'S RIGHT, JOANIE. AND TO PROTECT THEIR IDENTITIES, EACH WOMAN HAS BEEN SPRAYED BLACK!
SPRAYED BLACK?

SORRY, MISS. COMIX TECHNOLOGY IS A LITTLE PRIMITIVE.
THIS COMES OFF, RIGHT?

SENATOR PACKWOOD THEN GRABBED ME BY THE ARMS AND KISSED ME, FORCING HIS TONGUE INTO MY MOUTH...

PACKWOOD PINNED ME TO THE WALL AND KISSED ME. THEN I FELT THE TONGUE COMING...

HE HELD ME BY THE HAIR AND KISSED ME, FORCING HIS TONGUE INTO MY MOUTH...

THERE'S LIKE, A PATTERN HERE, ISN'T THERE?
UH-HUH. DID YOU GET THE DAMAGE DEPOSIT?

IT WAS IN HIS OFFICE IN THE SENATE BUILDING...

SENATOR PACKWOOD GRABBED ME AND PUSHED ME AGAINST THE WALL.

HE BENT ME BACKWARD AND FONDLED ME...
HOLD IT, HOLD IT!
©B Trudeau

WHAT?
YOU'RE A LITTLE NERVOUS, AREN'T YOU, MA'AM?
BETTER USE THIS BALLOON.

OH, NO, IT'S ALREADY FRIDAY AND WE STILL HAVE 12 WITNESSES LEFT!
HMM... I'LL SEE WHAT I CAN DO TO FIT 'EM IN...

HE GRABBED ME BY THE SHOULDERS AND KISSED ME ON THE...
AND THEN FORCED HIS TONGUE...
PUSHED ME ON COUCH INTO TONGUE MOUTH!
ASKED ME TO MAKE LOVE IN THE...
THEN
PINNED ME AGAINST THE WALL AND FONDLED ME WITH...
THEN HE UBBED WITH LEG ORCED ONGUE MOUTH!
FORCIBLY PULLED MY...
IN LEG TO SKIRT!
©B Trudeau
HAVE YOU CONSIDERED BOOKING A SUNDAY?
NO. THESE WOMEN HAVE FAMILIES.

WELL, THAT BRINGS US TO THE END OF OUR TESTIMONY. THERE WILL BE NO ALAN SIMPSON-STYLE GRILLING OF THE VICTIMS ABOUT THEIR PRIVATE LIVES.

AS THE LAW NOW RECOGNIZES, ASKING A SEXUAL ABUSE VICTIM ABOUT HER PAST BEHAVIOR IS AS RELEVANT AS ASKING A ROBBERY VICTIM IF HE'S A SPENDTHRIFT. THE ISSUE IS CONSENT!

BEFORE WE LEAVE, WE'D LIKE TO THANK OUR HOSTS FOR MAKING THIS VENUE AVAILABLE TO US. THEY WERE MOST GENEROUS.
©B Trudeau

HEY, IT WAS OUR PLEASURE!
I DUNNO, I COULD'VE DONE WITHOUT THE TONGUE STUFF.

J.J.!
HEY, STRANGER!

WE WERE IN THE NEIGHBORHOOD AND THOUGHT WE'D DROP BY! IF YOU'RE NOT TOO BUSY, I'D LOVE TO HANG AND PICK YOUR BRAIN...

I'M THINKING SERIOUSLY OF GETTING INTO THE MOVIE BUSINESS! I THOUGHT MAYBE YOU COULD GIVE ME AN INSIDER'S TAKE!

BACK UP. WHAT'S THE DEAL WITH THE ADULTERY?
OH, MIKE! IS **THAT** WHAT HE'S CALLING IT?

J.J., I DON'T KNOW **WHAT** YOU THINK YOU'RE DOING!

I CAN'T **BELIEVE** YOU WOULD RUN OUT ON POOR, SWEET, ADORABLE MIKE JUST TO BE WITH SOME... SOME...

IS THAT HIM OVER THERE?
UH-HUH.

ACTUALLY, HE **IS** PRETTY HOT.
THANKS. I GET A LOT OF THAT.

I HOPE YOU GUYS DON'T MIND OUR DROPPING IN LIKE THIS. I KNOW WE SHOULD HAVE CALLED AHEAD...

UM...B.D.? GUESS WHO'S HERE! J.J. AND HER FRIEND ZEKE!

YEAH, RIGHT. LIKE THAT EVIL LITTLE BIMBO AND HER SLEAZEBAG BOYFRIEND WOULD **DARE** SHOW THEIR FACES AROUND ANY OF MIKE'S FRIENDS!

HE CAN'T BELIEVE YOU'RE HERE.
ME, NEITHER. BUT I COULD GET USED TO THIS, MAN.

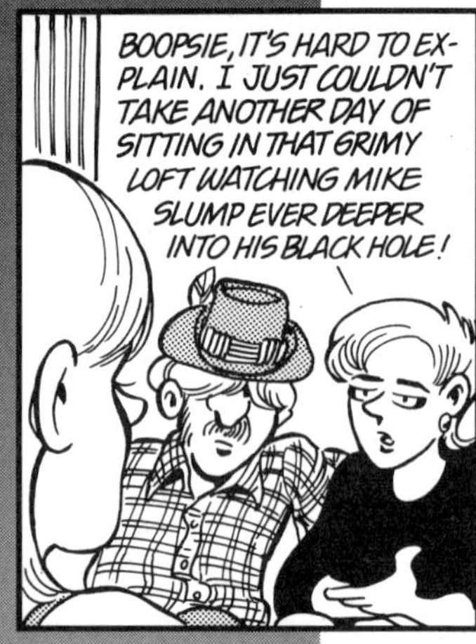
BOOPSIE, IT'S HARD TO EXPLAIN. I JUST COULDN'T TAKE ANOTHER DAY OF SITTING IN THAT GRIMY LOFT WATCHING MIKE SLUMP EVER DEEPER INTO HIS BLACK HOLE!

TOO BAD. BECAUSE TODAY HE'S LIVING THE SWEET LIFE IN SEATTLE, HEAD OF MARKETING FOR A SOFTWARE COMPANY AND HAULING DOWN A HUGE SALARY!

OH.

WELL, LA-DEE-DAH!
LIKE WHAT, SIX FIGURES?

ZEKE, HAVE YOU GUYS REALLY THOUGHT THROUGH THE CONSEQUENCES OF YOUR ACTIONS?
OF COURSE WE HAVE, MAN.

BUT IT'S NOT LIKE IT'S THE END OF THE WORLD IF IT DOESN'T WORK OUT. HELL, IF J.J. AND I DON'T MAKE IT, MAYBE I'LL COME BACK AND LOOK YOU UP, OKAY?

UM... THANKS FOR THE LOVELY OFFER, ZEKE, BUT I'M MARRIED.
SO WHAT? SO WAS J.J.!

THIS IS A REPULSIVE HUMAN BEING.
I KNEW YOU'D GET JEALOUS! MAYBE WE SHOULD JUST GO.

BOOPSIE HAS SOME NERVE, DISSING THE MAN I LOVE!
I KNEW THAT CHICK WAS BAD NEWS THE MOMENT I LAID EYES ON HER...

SOME WOMEN THINK THAT JUST BECAUSE THEY'RE BABES, THAT MAKES THEM SPECIAL, KNOW WHAT I MEAN?

YOU HIT ON HER, DIDN'T YOU?
WELL, JUST TO BE POLITE. THERE WAS A VIBE, MAN.

OH, MY GOD... IT'S YOU!
YES, MA'AM. GOOD MORNING.

HAROLD! COME HERE! QUICK!
I'M CANVASSING THE NEIGHBORHOOD. I WONDER IF I COULD ASK YOU A FEW QUESTIONS.

WELL, I'LL BE...
CAN YOU BELIEVE IT?
WHERE WERE YOU FOLKS THE NIGHT OF JUNE 12, 1994?

O.J. SIMPSON – PRIVATE INVESTIGATOR.
HMM... CAN'T RECALL...
ARE WE SUSPECTS? HOW EXCITING?
COULD YOU TRY ON THIS GLOVE, PLEASE, MA'AM?

O.J. SIMPSON, PRIVATE INVESTIGATOR, HITS THE STREETS.
SATISFIED?
YES, SIR. THANK YOU FOR YOUR COOPERATION.

I TOLD YOU THE GLOVE WOULDN'T FIT ME. I TAKE A SMALL.
IS THERE ANYONE ELSE LIVING IN THIS HOUSE, SIR?

JUST MY 80-YEAR-OLD FATHER.
COULD YOU ASK HIM TO TRY IT ON, TOO, SIR?

WELL, CERTAINLY. SHOULD I SCRAPE SOME DNA OFF HIS DENTURES, TOO?
IF IT'S NOT TOO MUCH TROUBLE.

NO KIDDING? YOU'RE REALLY LOOKING FOR YOUR WIFE'S MURDERER?
YES. MIND IF I ASK YOU A FEW QUESTIONS?

UM... WHY? AM I A SUSPECT?
WELL, YOU LIVE IN THE NEIGHBORHOOD. AND YOU OBVIOUSLY HAD MOTIVE.

I DID?
YES. LIKE A LOT OF BROTHERS, YOU PROBABLY RESENTED MY WHITE WIFE. IT COULD HAVE DRIVEN YOU TO MURDER!

WHO IS IT, HONEY?
INTERESTING THEORY.
YOU FOLKS HAVE A NICE DAY.

SORRY, MR. SIMPSON, IT DOESN'T FIT ANY-ONE IN THIS HOUSE.
THANKS ANYWAY, MA'AM.

IF YOU DON'T MIND MY ASKING, HAVE YOU BEEN SPENDING A LOT OF TIME LOOKING FOR THE REAL MURDERER?
ONLY EVERY MINUTE OF EVERY DAY!

WOW...

WHAT DO YOU DO AT NIGHT?
GRIEVE. PARTY. WHAT-EVER.

SORRY, JUICE — GRANDMA SAYS THE GLOVE DOESN'T FIT.
THANKS ANYWAY, SON...

SO HOW'S THE INVES-TIGATION GOING, JUICE? ANY LEADS?
NOT SO FAR.

THAT'S ROUGH, JUICE. I GUESS THE TRAIL'S PRETTY COLD, HUH?
AFRAID SO, SON.

WANT TO COME IN AND COL-LECT SOME FIBERS?
ABSOLUTELY NOT. YOU NEED A WARRANT FOR THAT.

GOOD EVENING FROM LOS ANGELES, WHERE THE POST-TRIAL O.J. WATCH CONTINUES.

TONIGHT ABC NEWS HAS LEARNED THAT MR. SIMPSON HAS JUST OBTAINED A PRIVATE INVESTIGATOR'S LICENSE...

...AND IS NOW COMBING BRENTWOOD IN SEARCH OF THE PERSON RESPONSIBLE FOR THE CRIMES OF WHICH HE WAS ACQUITTED. REACTION FROM NEIGHBORS HAS BEEN MIXED.

MURDERER!
WHERE? WHERE?

AH, TOBACCO! KING OF DRUGS!

...AND HE AIN'T JUST BLOWIN' SMOKE, FOLKS!

HEY, KID! WANT ME TO TEACH YOU HOW TO BLOW SMOKE RINGS?
NOT NOW, DAD, I'M TOO BUSY.
WRONG!
POP!
BEEP!
BING!

TAKE IT FROM ME, MR. BUTTS— YOU'RE NEVER TOO BUSY FOR A LESSON IN THE SMOKING ARTS—NO, SIR!
DINGADINGA!
BING!
POW!

...ESPECIALLY FROM A LEGENDARY "BAD BOY" LIKE THIS OL' TOMCAT! TALK ABOUT YOUR GLAMOUR!

BUT DON'T WORRY, LITTLE EARL— YOU'LL CATCH ON! WITH YOUR DAD AS ROLE MODEL, YOU'LL BE PUFFING UP A STORM BEFORE YOU CAN SAY "MALIGNANT NEOPLASM"!

WAS THAT YOUR IMAGINATION OR MINE?
YOURS. I'M TRYING TO HAVE A CHILDHOOD HERE.
BING!
©B Breathed

IS THAT A SLIGHT SAG?

HMM... MAYBE I NEED SURGERY...

B.D., DO YOU THINK I'VE STILL GOT THE CHOPS FOR THIS BUSINESS?
BOD-WISE? SURE. WHY?

I DUNNO. I'M NOT GETTING JUICY ROLES ANYMORE. MY LAST SHOWER SCENE WAS IN "CHUGALUG IV"...

...AND ALL THE GOOD HOOKER PARTS SEEM TO GO TO YOUNGER ACTRESSES. IT'S REALLY DEPRESSING.
WELL, LOOK, YOU **ARE** GETTING ON, BOOPSIE...

YOU'LL JUST HAVE TO ADJUST. PLAY ROLES WITH NO NUDITY. MOMS. AUNTS. PEOPLE LIKE THAT.

OH, B.D, DO YOU REALLY THINK SO? THAT WOULD MEAN THE END OF MY DREAM...
DREAM? WHAT DREAM?

OF ONE DAY WORKING WITH PHIL GRAMM.
LET IT GO, BABE, LET IT GO.
GBTrudeau

WILL THIS ALL BE MINE ONE DAY, DAD?
NOPE...

...UNLESS WE CAN GET THAT TWIT JOHN DENVER TO SELL OUT.

THE THING IS, SON, YOU GOT NO IDEA HOW HARD IT IS TO BE A PARENT TODAY...

JUST GIVING A KID A NORMAL UPBRINGING IS AN INCREDIBLE UNDERTAKING!
UH-HUH...

ANYWAY... HEY!... DID YOU HEAR THAT?
HEAR WHAT?

THAT!
SPROING!
WHOOSH!

BLAM!
BLAM!
CLANG!
WHOOPEE! AWESOME SHOOTIN', DAD!

ARE THEY GOOD TO EAT?
HAVEN'T A CLUE. I NEVER HIT ONE BEFORE.
©B Trudeau

WHAT'S UP, DAD?
THE CRISIS IS OVER!

THAT'S GREAT! WHAT CRISIS?
THE CRISIS OF CONFI-DENCE IN OUR FINE PRODUCT!

GOOD NEWS, FOLKS! THE DEFECTIVE CIG-ARETTE CRISIS IS OVER! THEY'VE ALL BEEN RECALLED!
WHEW!

WHY DID WE RECALL THEM? BECAUSE WE CARE! IT TORE US UP KNOW-ING THAT WE. HAD PLACED SMOKERS AT RISK!

IN FACT, PHILIP MORRIS NOW IN-VITES YOU TO JOIN US IN A MOMENT OF SILENCE FOR ALL OF THOSE WHO SUF-FERED SCRATCHY THROATS OR MILD DIZZINESS!

PSST! DAD! SHOULDN'T WE INCLUDE ALL THOSE WHO DIED, TOO?
THEY'RE FORMER CUSTOMERS. THIS IS FOR CURRENT CUSTOMERS!

OH...
OKAY, MOMENT'S OVER!
NO HARD FEELINGS, RIGHT?
NO WAY!

WHY ARE WE STOPPING, ZEKE?
TO CHECK OUT THE NIGHT SKY, MAN. WHAT ELSE?

YOU REALLY ARE HALF-STAR-CREATURE, HALF-SOMETHING ELSE, AREN'T YOU, ZEKE?
FOR SURE, MAN.

WE SHOULD MAKE SANTA FE TOMORROW, MAN...
I KNOW...

I WAS THINKING OF HAVING A SHOW THERE, ZEKE. MAYBE EXHIBIT THE HUBCAP PIECES I'VE BEEN WORKING ON...

I THINK THE SALES AND REVIEWS I COULD GET OUT OF THAT WOULD ESTABLISH ME AS A MAJOR REGIONAL ARTIST...

I COULD THEN PARLAY THAT INTO A DIRECTING CAREER, MAKING ACCLAIMED INDEPENDENT FILMS WITH STARS LIKE DE NIRO AND BRANDO, WHO'D WORK FOR FREE OUT OF RESPECT FOR MY BODY OF WORK.

HMM... SOUNDS SOLID.

IT'S GOOD TO HAVE A PLAN LIKE THAT, MAN.
HEY, IN THIS ECONOMY, ANYONE WHO DOESN'T IS A FOOL!

CHANGE-UP! CHANGE-UP!

BUT NOW THE BATTER WILL KNOW.
IT WAS JUST A SUGGEST-ION, DAD.
102

ENJOYING THE BALL GAME, SIR?
UH... YEAH. WHO ARE YOU?
HEY, BATTAH, BATTAH!
102

I'M VICE PRESIDENT OF MAR-KETING WITH THE TEAM, SIR. I JUST WANTED TO THANK YOU PERSONALLY FOR COM-ING OUT TO THE PARK TODAY!
WELL, YOUR 90% DISCOUNT MIGHT HAVE HAD SOMETHING TO DO WITH IT.

LIKE IT? WE WANTED TO MAKE THE BALL PARK EXPERIENCE AT-TRACTIVE TO FAMILIES AGAIN!
WE ALSO LIKED THE FREE HOT DOGS, BALLS AND PARKING.
SHOW HIM YOUR STUFF, PITCH!

WELL, IT'S THE LEAST MANAGEMENT CAN DO, SIR!
MANAGEMENT? WHAT ABOUT THE PLAYERS? THEY HAVE AS MUCH TO DO WITH THE DEATH OF BASEBALL AS YOU GUYS!
C'MON, BRIAN. PUT HIM AWAY!

QUITE RIGHT! WHY DON'T I SEND UP ONE OF OUR STARS TO PERSONALLY APOLOGIZE TO YOU!
WHICH ONE?
YOU CALL THAT A HEAT-ER? YOU STINK, BRIAN!

TAKE YOUR PICK, SIR!
UM...
HOW ABOUT THE PITCHER? HE'S NOT BUSY!
GB Trudeau

BUT WHICH ONE HAD AN AFFAIR FIRST?

INQUIRING MINDS NEED TO KNOW!

YOU KNOW, THIS RICHARD GERE-CINDY CRAWFORD SPLIT COULD BE MY FAVORITE SUMMER STORY...
49¢

HAVE THEY GOTTEN TO THE BOTTOM OF IT YET?
PRETTY MUCH...
Kellogg's

IT TURNS OUT CINDY WAS ON A PARTY GIRL TRACK. SHE LIKED TO STAY OUT ALL NIGHT AT THE CLUBS DRINKING TEQUILA WITH OTHER MODELS.
MOM K
SELF

BUT RICHARD WAS A BUD-DHIST—HE'D OUTGROWN ALL THAT. HE JUST WANTED TO STAY HOME AND MEDITATE AND SIP YAK MILK.

SO BASICALLY, CINDY LEFT RICHARD GERE BECAUSE HE WASN'T SHALLOW ENOUGH FOR HER.

WHOA... BEEN THERE!
YEAH, IT'S REASSUR-ING WHEN CELEBS HAVE THE SAME PROBLEMS YOU DO.
GBTrudeau

MMM... SMELL THAT CLEAN AIR...

I JUST WISH IT WERE WORTH THE REGULATORY BURDEN.

YOU KNOW, IF VOTERS HAVE SENT US ONE MESSAGE LOUD AND CLEAR...

...IT'S THAT THEY'RE TIRED OF GOVERNMENT INSPECTORS TELLING THEM WHAT TO EAT, DRINK AND BREATHE!

TAKE SPOILED MEAT— IT COSTS US 4,000 LIVES, 5 MILLION ILLNESSES AND OVER $3 BILLION IN MEDICAL EXPENSES YEARLY.

BUT DOES THAT JUSTIFY THE HORRIFIC REGULATORY BURDEN ON THE MEAT INDUSTRY? COULDN'T WE LIVE WITH 8,000 DEATHS? OR 12,000?

AMERICANS ARE **CRYING OUT** FOR COST-BENEFIT RATIOS THAT MAKE SENSE TO BUSINESS! IF I'M ELECTED, THEY'LL GET 'EM!

BOB DOLE FOR PRESIDENT.
BECAUSE WE ALL HAVE TO DIE OF SOMETHING.
GB Trudeau

"CONGRATULATIONS. YOU FOUND THE STUPID WIZARD."

THAT'S IT? THAT'S THE **WHOLE GAME**?

HEY, POP-O-RAMA! WHAT'S THIS NEW GAME ON THE LAPTOP?
TAP! TAP!

IT'S CALLED "WIZ-TRON," BABE. IT'S OUR BIG CHRISTMAS CD-ROM RELEASE. WHAT DO YOU THINK?

WELL, THE INTERFACE IS A BIT POKEY, AND THE O/S DOES A MELTDOWN EVERY TIME I MULTI-TASK THE NAVIGATOR...

ALSO, THE GRAPHICS ARE PRE-MYSTIAN — VERY 1991. AND THE STORY ACTION IS PREDICTABLE. I FOUND THE WIZARD IN TEN MINUTES.

TEN MINUTES?
YEAH. IT MIGHT WORK FOR YOUNGER KIDS, THOUGH. LIKE TWO-OR-THREE-YEAR-OLDS.

WE'VE GOT A PROBLEM.
HOW BIG? WE JUST SHIPPED A MILLION UNITS.
© B Trudeau

BOY... THIS TAKES ME BACK...
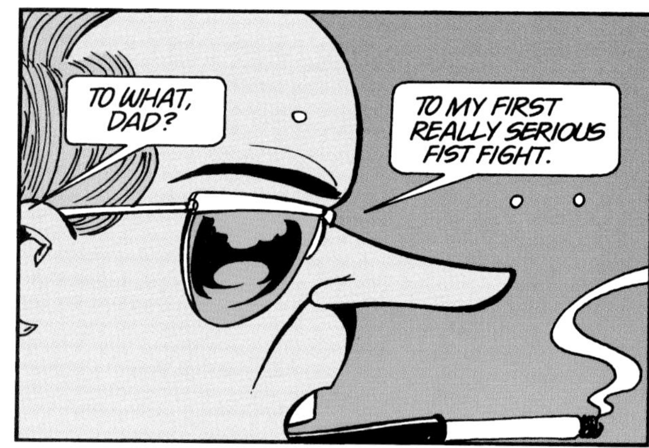
TO WHAT, DAD?
TO MY FIRST REALLY SERIOUS FIST FIGHT.

OF ALL THE SUMMER-TIME RITUALS...
YO! TWO OVER HERE!
HOT DOGS! HOT DOGS HERE!

...THAT BOND A FATHER TO A SON...
HEY, NUMBER 5! YOU STINK!
YOU TELL HIM, SON!

... ON THE EDGE OF YOUNG MANHOOD...
GO, BOOMER, GO!
DIG IT OUT! DIG IT OUT!

... NONE IS SO SWEET...
OH, NOOO!

... SO AFFECTIONATELY HELD IN MEMORY...
YOU BUM! YOU BUM!
YOU'RE A LOSER, BOOMER! A BIG LOSER!

... AS HIS FIRST DAY AT THE TRACK.
DAD, CAN I HAVE ANOTHER BEER?
NO. WE'RE OUT OF MONEY.

YOU ASK HIM.
NO, YOU.

OKAY, BUT YOU HAVE TO ASK FOLLOW-UP.
I'LL BE RIGHT BEHIND YOU.
ME, TOO.

MR. SPEAKER, AS YOU INCH CLOSER TO A RUN AT THE PRESIDENCY, YOUR IMAGE AS A CHAMPION OF FAMILY VALUES HAS COME UNDER SEVERE ATTACK...

NOT ONLY DOES IT APPEAR YOU WERE A DEADBEAT DAD, BUT IT NOW SEEMS YOU WERE ROUTINELY UNFAITHFUL TO YOUR FIRST WIFE BEFORE LEAVING HER...

LOOK, FIRST OFF, ALL THESE ACCUSATIONS ARE COMING FROM DISGRUNTLED CAMPAIGN WORKERS, DISGRUNTLED EMPLOYEES, DISGRUNTLED FRIENDS AND DISGRUNTLED RELATIVES...

SECONDLY, I NEVER SAID I WAS PERFECT. WHO IS, IN THIS DAY AND AGE? PHIL GRAMM LEFT HIS FIRST WIFE. BOB DOLE LEFT HIS. SAME WITH PETE WILSON.

NOW, THESE MEN ARE ALL GREAT AMERICANS. SO WHAT DOES THAT TELL YOU? MAYBE THE PROBLEM ISN'T WITH US— MAYBE THE PROBLEM IS WITH FIRST WIVES!

ALL FIRST WIVES?
THEY EXPECT SO **MUCH**! SECOND WIVES ARE MORE REALISTIC!
GB Trudeau

"GO: WHITE HOUSE."

WONDER IF HE'S HOME...
CLIK!
CLIK!

Online with
The President

WHAT DO YOU THINK, MIKE? OUR BROWSER LINKS YOU WITH THE BIG GUY FASTER AND CHEAPER THAN ANY OTHER PRO-GRAM!

UM...SURE. BUT THERE'S NO THERE THERE, BERN.
WHY? BECAUSE HE'S AN ICON? DON'T BE FOOLED BY THAT...

THE WAFFLE'S NOT JUST A FILE ICON—IT'S A **FOLDER** ICON, THE SUM OF **MANY** PARTS! THERE'S MORE TO HIM THAN APPEARS!
Welcome!

REALLY?
CLICK ON HIM AND SEE FOR YOURSELF!

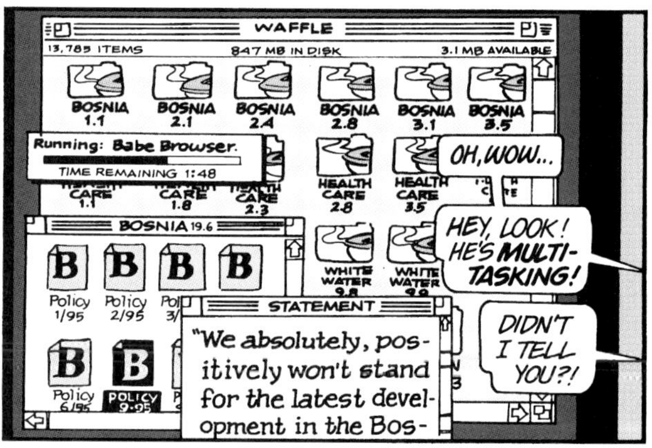
WAFFLE
13,785 ITEMS
847 MB IN DISK
3.1 MB AVAILABLE
BOSNIA 1.1
BOSNIA 2.1
BOSNIA 2.4
BOSNIA 2.8
BOSNIA 3.1
BOSNIA 3.5
Running: Babe Browser.
TIME REMAINING 1:48
CARE 1.1
CARE 1.8
CARE 2.3
HEALTH CARE 2.8
HEALTH CARE 3.5
BOSNIA 19.6
Policy 1/95
Policy 2/95
Policy 6/95
POLICY 9·95
WHITE WATER
WHITE WATER
STATEMENT
"We absolutely, pos-itively won't stand for the latest devel-opment in the Bos-
OH, WOW...
HEY, LOOK! HE'S **MULTI-TASKING!**
DIDN'T I TELL YOU?!

HEY, DAD! TIME TO GET UP! YOU GOTTA TAKE ME TO SCHOOL!
RIGHT. I'M UP. NO PROBLEM.

NEED ANY HELP?
NO, I CAN MANAGE...
WHERE AM I?

HEY, DAD?

HMM?
TODAY'S THE FIRST DAY OF SCHOOL. WHEN WE GET THERE, DO YOU THINK YOU COULD ACT... NORMAL?

NORMAL? OF COURSE I'LL ACT NORMAL! THINK I'D EMBARRASS MY OWN KID?
WELL...
WANT

BELIEVE ME, I KNOW WHAT IT'S LIKE TO BE HUMILIATED BY YOUR OLD MAN IN FRONT OF YOUR FRIENDS!
YOU DO?

TRUST ME ON THIS ONE, BOY. C'MON, IT'S LATE—LET'S HIT THE ROAD.
I'M READY.

OKAY, HOW DO YOU DRIVE THIS THING?
WHAT THING?

"TO THINE OWN SELF BE TRUE."
GOOD STUFF, YEATS.

IT'S A COMMERCIAL, ZEKE.
I KNEW THAT.

WOW... LOOK AT THAT! THE RIVER'S JUST THIS TINY RIBBON OF SILVER NOW...

AIN'T THE ALL-TERRAIN LIFE GREAT, MAN?
YEAH. HOW FAR YOU FIGURE WE ARE FROM CIVILIZATION?

WELL, WE'VE BEEN HIKING FOR TWO DAYS. THERE CAN'T BE ANYONE WITHIN 30 MILES OF US...

HELLO?
HUH?...

EXCUSE ME? ARE YOU J.J. CAUCUS?
UH... YEAH. WHO ARE YOU?

CONSIDER YOURSELF SERVED. HAVE A NICE DIVORCE.
WHAT!
WHOA... YOU'RE GOOD, MAN. WANT A BEER?
GB Trudeau

WONDER HOW BOB DOLE'S MAKING OUT...

NO, I DON'T... NOT REALLY...

DOLE! DOLE!! DOLE!!
THANK YOU, THANK YOU VERY MUCH...

YOU KNOW, I GET ASKED A LOT, "SENATOR, WHY DO YOU WANT TO BE PRESI-DENT? HAVEN'T YOU GIVEN ENOUGH TO YOUR COUNTRY?"

WELL, THE ANSWER IS YES, I HAVE! AND THAT'S WHY I WANT TO BE PRESIDENT – I'VE **EARNED** IT! I'VE BEEN THERE! I KNOW WHAT LEADER-SHIP'S ALL ABOUT!

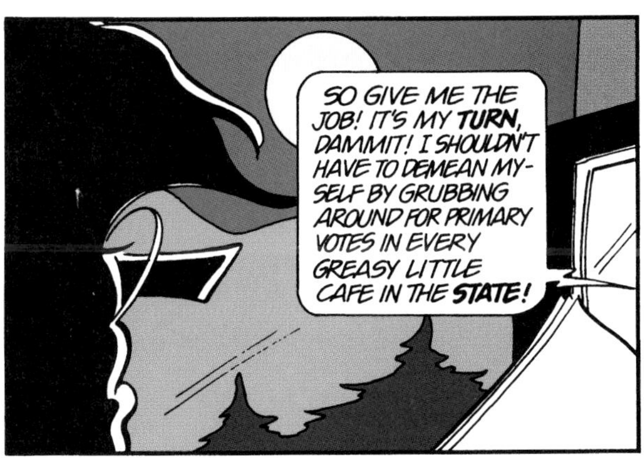
SO GIVE ME THE JOB! IT'S MY **TURN**, DAMMIT! I SHOULDN'T HAVE TO DEMEAN MY-SELF BY GRUBBING AROUND FOR PRIMARY VOTES IN EVERY GREASY LITTLE CAFE IN THE **STATE**!

OOPS.
GRAMM! GRAMM! GRAMM!

WANT TO GO HUNTING TODAY, KID?
YEAH! COOL!

BE BACK BE-FORE MIDNIGHT, OKAY?
AW, DAD!

DAD, DID YOU KNOW THE F.B.I. AND THE A.T.F. HAVE A MAS-TER PLAN FOR TOTAL GUN CONTROL?
NO KIDDING? WHERE'D YOU PICK THAT UP?

ONE OF THOSE MAGA-ZINES YOU GET. AP-PARENTLY THERE'S THIS WHOLE PLOT...

IF YOU WANT MY OPINION, I THINK WE SHOULD START STOCKPILING NOW. WE COULD PACK GUNS INTO OIL DRUMS AND THEN BURY 'EM OUT BACK!

YOU JUST CAN'T TRUST ANYONE TODAY, CAN YOU, DAD? THE GOV-ERNMENT, COPS, TEACHERS, BU-REAUCRATS – THEY ALL WANT TO TAKE YOUR FREEDOM AWAY! THEY'RE ALL SCUM WHO DE-SERVE TO DIE, RIGHT, DAD?

DAD?

DAD?... ARE YOU CRYING?
I'M OKAY...
IT'S JUST I'M SO DAMN PROUD OF YOU.
GBTrudeau

SIR? SIR, WAKE UP! THE INSPECTOR FROM CHILD SERVICES IS HERE!
MMPH! SNORT!

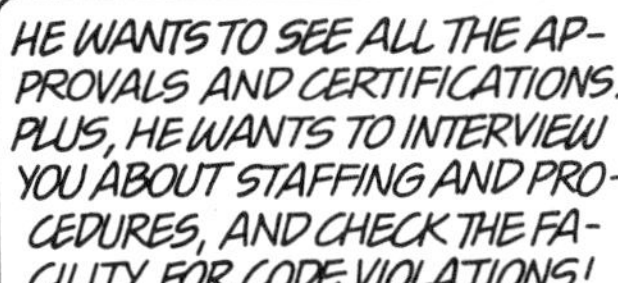
HE WANTS TO SEE ALL THE APPROVALS AND CERTIFICATIONS. PLUS, HE WANTS TO INTERVIEW YOU ABOUT STAFFING AND PROCEDURES, AND CHECK THE FACILITY FOR CODE VIOLATIONS!

HONEY, HAVE YOU EVER CONSIDERED USING SUBTITLES?
I'LL HOLD HIM OFF AS LONG AS I CAN.
GB Trudeau

SIR, YOU BETTER HURRY. THE CHILD WELFARE MAN IS WAITING...
THIS IS AN **OUTRAGE**!

IT'S **EXACTLY** THE KIND OF GOVERNMENT INTRUSION THAT NEWT-BOY **SWORE** HE'D DO AWAY WITH!

BESIDES, WHY **US?** WE USE **NOTHING** IN OUR PRODUCTS BUT CHOICE, GRADE-A **PORK**!

UM... FYI, SIR, WE'RE RUNNING AN ORPHANAGE NOW.
I KNEW THAT. FOR PIGS?
GB Trudeau

OKAY, BUD—WHAT'S SO IMPORTANT I HAD TO INTERRUPT OUR DAILY PRAYER BREAKFAST?

MR. DUKE? I'M KEVIN DEVILLE FROM CHILD WELFARE SERVICES.
YEAH? SO? WHAT'S THE PROBLEM?

WE RECEIVED AN ANONYMOUS CALL ALERTING US TO NUMEROUS CODE VIOLATIONS OUT HERE.
WHAT? THAT'S IMPOSSIBLE! WE DON'T LET THE KIDS USE THE PHONE...

SHE HAD A CHINESE ACCENT.
YOU DON'T SAY.
MANDARIN OR CANTONESE?
GB Trudeau

OKAY, LET'S SEE THE SLEEPING QUARTERS...
STRAIGHT AHEAD.

HOW MANY KIDS ARE IN THIS ROOM?
I DUNNO... 35?

35 KIDS IN ONE ROOM?
IT'S PLENTY BIG ENOUGH, SIR. IN CHINA, WE HOUSE TWICE THIS MANY CHILDREN IN A ROOM THIS SIZE.

IN CHINA, YOU KILL THE GIRLS.
YOU PUT TO BOYS TOGETHER?
I WITH-DRAW THE COMMENT.

HOW MANY STEPS YOU MISSING THERE? THREE? FOUR?
YOU NEED ME TO DO THE MATH FOR YOU?

MR. DUKE, I'VE NEVER SEEN A CHILD CARE FA-CILITY IN SUCH POOR CONDITION!
NO KID-DING? NEVER?
Nothin' But Orphans

AND YOU'RE LOW ON EVERYTHING— DISINFECTANTS, SOAP, BAND-AIDS...
BUDGET CUTS! WHAT CAN I DO?

PLENTY OF DUCT TAPE, THOUGH, I SEE...
A NANNY'S BEST FRIEND! NOTICE HOW QUIET IT IS?
ACME
ACME

WELL, YOUR BOOK-KEEPING IS AS BAD AS EVERYTHING ELSE HERE. WHAT'S THIS BIG CASH DISBURSE-MENTS ACCOUNT FOR?

TO MAKE NEW FRIENDS, LIKE YOURSELF, FOR INSTANCE. WE'D LIKE YOU TO BE OUR FRIEND.
OH, REALLY?

REALLY! TAKE WHAT-EVER YOU NEED. A GUY ON A GOVERNMENT SALA-RY COULD PROBABLY USE A FEW EXTRA... EXTRA... UM... WHAT ARE YOU DOING?

I'M ABOUT TO HAVE A REALLY BAD DAY, AREN'T I?
YEAH.
SHERIFF'S OFFICE.

YOU TRIED TO BRIBE THE INSPECTOR? WHAT WERE YOU THINKING, SIR?
I WAS THINKING IT USUALLY WORKS. NOW I GOTTA DEAL WITH THE DAMN SHERIFF...
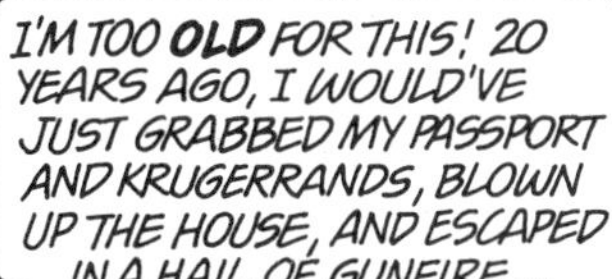
I'M TOO OLD FOR THIS! 20 YEARS AGO, I WOULD'VE JUST GRABBED MY PASSPORT AND KRUGERRANDS, BLOWN UP THE HOUSE, AND ESCAPED IN A HAIL OF GUNFIRE...

BUT NOW... NOW... SIGH...

NOW WHAT, SIR?
NOW I JUST WANT TO TAKE A NAP.
WANT ME TO BLOW UP THE HOUSE FOR YOU, DAD?
G.B. Trudeau

WHAT'S UP, EARL? WHY THE EMERGENCY MEETING?
BIG TROUBLE, EVERYONE! THE SHERIFF'S COMING OUT AFTER DUKE!

WE CAN'T LET THIS HAPPEN! DUKE MEANS EVERYTHING TO US, AND WE HAVE TO MAKE IT CLEAR TO THE SHERIFF THAT IF HE WANTS TO TAKE DUKE, HE'S GONNA HAVE TO GET PAST US FIRST! ANY QUESTIONS?

G.B. Trudeau

WHO'S DUKE?
THE DRUNK GUY OUT BACK.
WHAT DO YOU SAY— ARE YOU WITH ME?

DAD? I'VE SPOKEN TO THE OTHER KIDS AND WE'RE ALL BEHIND YOU!

WE'RE NOT GOING TO LET THE SHERIFF TAKE YOU, DAD! NO WAY! I GOT EVERYONE PUMPED, TOTALLY FIRED!

SIR? THE SHERIFF JUST PULLED UP...
GOOD GOD, ALREADY? WHERE ARE THE KIDS?
G.B. Trudeau

NOT TO WORRY. THEY ESCAPED OUT THE BACK.
PROBABLY TO FLANK HIM.
GOOD WORK, EARL.

IT'S ALL BO-GUS, SHERIFF! SOME BONE-HEAD BUREAU-CRAT WHO...
LOOK, DUKE, YOU KNOW ME—NORMAL-LY I DON'T GIVE A FLY-ING FIG...

BUT YOU GOT KIDS OUT HERE! AND THIS GUY'S LISTING 143 SERIOUS CODE VIOLATIONS!
HEY, THE KIDS DON'T CARE! ASK 'EM!

WELL, THAT'S NOT THE WORST OF IT. HE ALSO SAYS YOU TRIED TO BRIBE HIM.
HE DID?
ZZT!

YEAH. SO WHAT GIVES? YOU'VE NEVER OFFERED ME A BRIBE!
SHERIFF, YOU'RE LIKE FAMILY! IT NEVER SEEMED NECESSARY!

OKAY, MAYBE I DID TRY TO GREASE THE WHEELS A LITTLE—WAS THAT SO WRONG?

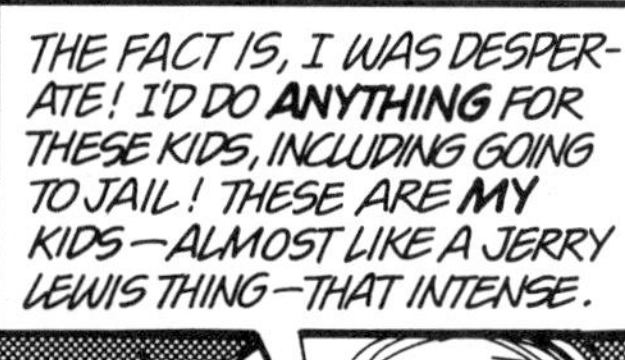
THE FACT IS, I WAS DESPER-ATE! I'D DO ANYTHING FOR THESE KIDS, INCLUDING GOING TO JAIL! THESE ARE MY KIDS—ALMOST LIKE A JERRY LEWIS THING—THAT INTENSE.

UH-HUH. WELL, LOOK, DUKE, I'M TOO BUSY TO BOOK YOU RIGHT NOW, SO WHY DON'T YOU JUST VANISH BEFORE I GET BACK, OKAY?
VAN-ISH?

THREE-DAY HEAD START SEEM FAIR?
SIX. I GOTTA DUMP THE KIDS.

HOW LONG WILL YOU BE GONE, DAD?
THERE'S NO TELLING. I'LL BE A FUGITIVE FROM JUSTICE.

CAN'T I COME WITH YOU? WE COULD BE OUTLAWS TOGETHER!
HOW YOU FIG-URE? I'M THE ONLY ONE IN TROUBLE!

RIGHT, BUT I'D BE HELP-ING YOU! THAT WOULD MAKE ME AN ACCES-SORY!
WELL, I GUESS THAT'S RIGHT.

AHEM. WHAT ABOUT HIS ED-UCATION?
HEY... WHO ASKED YOU?
I'LL JUST PICK HIM UP SOME CD-ROM'S OR SOME-THING.

ANYWAY, AFTER WE GET BACK TO ASPEN, I'M **DEF-INITELY** GOING TO GET A SHOW OF NEW STUFF OFF THE GROUND...

I MIGHT THEN PARLAY THE RECOGNITION FROM THAT IN-TO A BOOK OR A MOVIE OR SOMETHING. OR I MIGHT START A MAGAZINE, Y'KNOW?

ZEKE, YOU'VE BEEN AWFULLY QUIET THE LAST FEW MILES. IS SOMETHING WRONG?

NO...WELL, IT'S JUST TOUGH LIVING IN YOUR SHADOW, MAN.
REALLY? SEE, NOW, MIKE WOULD **NEVER** ADMIT THAT.
GB Trudeau

WHOA... WHAT'S **THIS** GUY'S STORY?
THE JERK'S DRIVING ON THE WRONG SIDE...

OH, MY **GOD**... LOOK OUT! **LOOK OUT!**
BEEP!
BEEP!

AIEEE!

WOW... THINK THEY'RE ALL RIGHT?
WHO?
GB Trudeau

MY GOD... WHAT HAPPENED?
SOMEONE RAN US OFF THE ROAD... YOU OKAY?

I DUNNO... MY HEAD'S BLEEDING...
WELL, DON'T MOVE UNTIL THE PARA-MEDICS GET HERE.

YOU KNOW, THAT MANIAC LOOKED FAMILIAR—**VERY** FAMILIAR...

I'M GOING TO PASS OUT NOW.
OKAY, MAN. I'LL HOLD DOWN THE FORT.
GB Trudeau

EARL, I'M A FUGITIVE FROM JUSTICE—I DON'T HAVE TIME FOR THIS!
DAD, YOU RAN THEM OFF THE ROAD! YOU HAVE TO GO SEE IF THEY'RE OKAY!

HURRY, DAD! THEY COULD BE BLEED-ING TO DEATH!
IT'D BE JUST MY LUCK...

OKAY, DOGMEAT, WHAT THE HELL WERE YOU DOING ON MY SIDE OF THE... ACK! IT'S YOU!

SON! BRING DOWN MY GUN!
I KNEW IT! I KNEW IT WAS DUKE!

LOOK, BRENNER, I HAVEN'T GOT TIME TO DEAL WITH THIS, BUT I'LL CALL 911, OKAY?

LOOK, JERK-FACE, IF YOU HADN'T BEEN ON THE WRONG SIDE OF THE ROAD, THIS WOULDN'T HAVE HAPPENED! THIS IS BERMUDA, Y'KNOW!
DON'T DO US ANY FA-VORS, DUKE! COUGH!

YOU MISERABLE, COKE-ADDLED, OLD FOOL! THIS ISN'T BERMUDA—IT'S FREAKIN' COLORADO!
BEEP! BEEP! BEEP!

HE'S RIGHT, DAD. WE WERE JUST HEADED FOR BER-MUDA.
BY CAR? THAT MAKES NO SENSE!
911. PLEASE HOLD.

DAD, DO YOU THINK THE PARAMEDICS WILL GET THERE IN TIME?

I MEAN, THAT LADY HAD A PRETTY BAD CUT ON HER HEAD. I HOPE SHE DOESN'T LOSE TOO MUCH BLOOD...

'COURSE, THE HOSPI-TAL IN ASPEN IS SUP-POSED TO BE PRETTY GOOD, RIGHT? THAT'S WHAT I HEARD. RIGHT?

UH... DAD? HELLO?
DAMN, I HATE LEAVING WITNESS-ES! IT'S JUST UN-PROFESSIONAL!

CLEAR CUBICLE FOUR!
OOH... WHERE AM I?

YOU'RE AT THE HOSPITAL, HONEY. YOU WERE IN AN ACCIDENT.
EDDIE! HEAD CASE! PAGE RIFKIN!
ACCIDENT?

WAIT A MINUTE... MY BOY-FRIEND...
HE'S FINE. HE'S JUST CHECKING YOU IN.

I'M SORRY, SIR–WE DON'T ACCEPT BLACK AND DECKER WARRANTY CARDS.
GET OUTA HERE.

HEY, LITTLE LADY. HOW MANY FINGERS?

TWO. ARE THOSE EYES FOR REAL?
WHAT DO YOU MEAN?

YOU'RE ONLY THE MOST BEAUTIFUL MAN I'VE EVER SEEN IN MY LIFE!
IS THAT RIGHT?

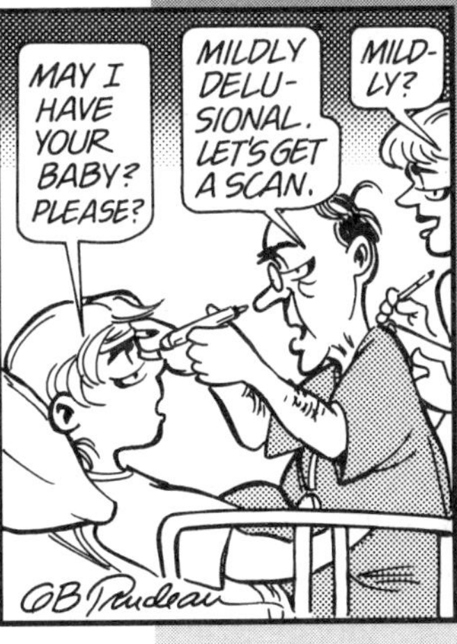
MAY I HAVE YOUR BABY? PLEASE?
MILDLY DELU-SIONAL. LET'S GET A SCAN.
MILD-LY?

MR. DOONES-BURY?
UH... YEAH, OVER HERE!

I'M DR. RIFKIN. I JUST FINISHED TREATING YOUR WIFE...
HOW IS SHE, MAN?

SHE'LL BE FINE. I SEWED UP THE HEAD LACERATIONS AND RAN SOME TESTS. BUT I WANT TO KEEP HER FOR OBSERVATION.
HOW COME?

SHE MADE A PASS AT ME.
SAY NO MORE, MAN.

THE DOCTOR SAYS YOU'RE GONNA BE ALL RIGHT, MAN. HOW YOU FEELING?

A LITTLE SHAKY. I KEEP SEEING THAT CAR COMING AT US, AND THEN US FLYING OFF INTO THAT GORGE, FALLING... FALLING...

FALL...

SORRY, BABE... I'M PASSING OUT AGAIN...
NO PROBLEM. MIND IF I GO TO A MOVIE?
GB Trudeau

MRS. DOONESBURY? I'M DR. STICKLER. ANY NAUSEA TODAY? HOW ABOUT NUMBNESS?

MRS. DOONESBURY? I'M DR. GREEN. ANY NAUSEA TODAY? OR NUMBNESS?
GOOD. NO CHILLS? DIZZY SPELLS?
NO, I...

NO. AS I JUST TOLD...
OKAY, DEEP BREATH.
HOW ABOUT CHILLS?
ANY NAUSEA TODAY, MISS?
OR NUMBNESS?
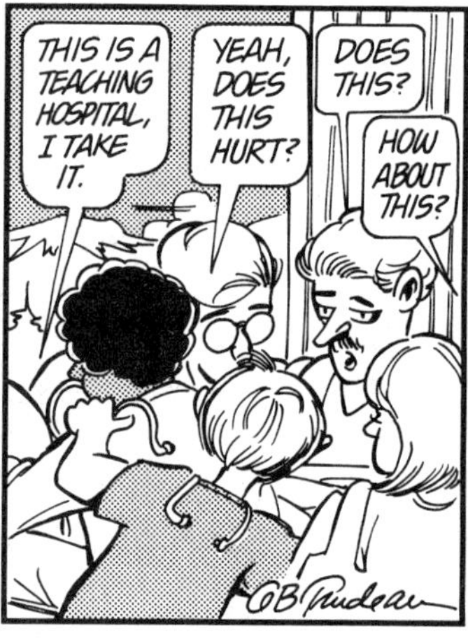
THIS IS A TEACHING HOSPITAL, I TAKE IT.
YEAH, DOES THIS HURT?
DOES THIS?
HOW ABOUT THIS?
GB Trudeau

YOU KNOW WHAT ONE OF THE DOCTORS HERE TOLD ME, MAN? HE SAID DURING SKI SEASON, THEY ADMIT 100 PEOPLE A DAY HERE — ALL TORN UP ON THE MOUNTAIN!
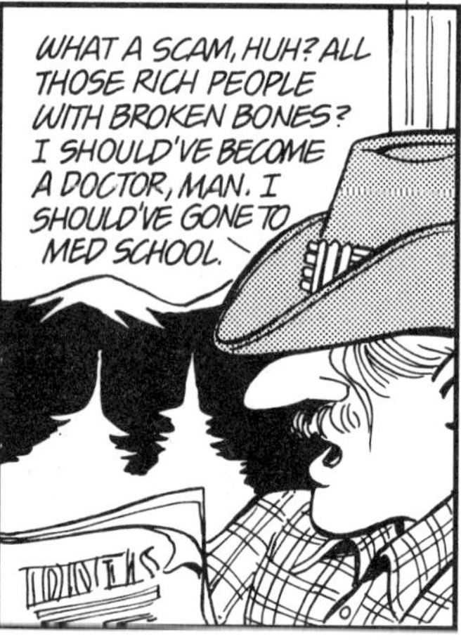
WHAT A SCAM, HUH? ALL THOSE RICH PEOPLE WITH BROKEN BONES? I SHOULD'VE BECOME A DOCTOR, MAN. I SHOULD'VE GONE TO MED SCHOOL.

MED SCHOOL?
YEAH.

BABE, YOU SHOULD HAVE GONE TO HIGH SCHOOL.
NAH, HIGH SCHOOL'S FOR LOSERS. I MADE THE RIGHT CHOICE THERE.
GB Trudeau

MARKETING, THIS IS MIKE.
YEAH, MIKE, THIS IS ZEKE, J.J.'S BOY-FRIEND, OKAY?

IT CERTAINLY IS **NOT** OKAY, YOU...
HEY, CHILL, MAN, THIS IS IMPOR-TANT. J.J. WAS IN A CAR ACCI-DENT...

WHAT?
AT FIRST SHE WAS FINE. THEY GOT HER STABILIZED. BUT THEN LAST NIGHT, WITHOUT WARN-ING, SHE... SHE...

J.J.'S DEAD, ISN'T SHE?
NO, JUST A COMA, MAN. BUT I WAS WONDERING IF YOU COULD HELP WITH THE TAB.

ZEKE?
OH, HEY, MAN! THANKS FOR COMING...

HOW IS SHE?
STILL IN A COMA, MAN...

BUT I KNOW IT'S GOING TO HELP HER JUST HAVING YOU HERE. IT CERTAINLY MEANS THE **WORLD** TO ME, MAN...

IT DOES?
HELL, YES! HEY, YOU BROUGHT YOUR INSUR-ANCE CARD, DIDN'T YOU?

J.J.?

J.J.? IT'S ME, BABE — MIKE...

MIKE, YOUR HUSBAND OF 13 YEARS, NOT SOME SLEAZEBUCKET WHO PICKED YOU UP AND TRASHED YOUR LIFE...

BACK OFF, MAN. YOU'RE CONFUS-ING HER.
AM I, J.J.? JUST BREATHE IF THE AN-SWER'S NO.

SHE'S BEEN LIKE THIS FOR TWO DAYS, MAN. I HAVEN'T LEFT HER SIDE...

WELL, ONCE FOR A MOVIE. AND ONCE TO GET BEER. BUT OTHER THAN THAT, I'VE BEEN HERE FOR HER.

EXCUSE ME, BUT VISITING HOURS ARE OVER, MR. DOONESBURY.
THANKS, MAN.

MR. WHO?
YOU CAN HAVE IT BACK, MAN. IT'S A DORKY NAME ANYWAY.

J.J., WHY DID IT COME TO THIS? WHY DID ANY OF THIS HAVE TO HAPPEN?

WE LOVED EACH OTHER. WE BUILT A LIFE TOGETHER. WE MADE A FAMILY. WHY DID YOU RUN AWAY FROM ALL THAT? I DON'T UNDERSTAND...

IRONIC, ISN'T IT, MAN?
WHAT IS, ZEKE?

SHE WAS NEVER MUCH OF A LISTENER BEFORE.
ZEKE, GO HIT ON A NURSE OR SOMETHING, WOULD YOU?

SO WHAT DO YOU THINK, DOCTOR? IS SHE GOING TO COME OUT OF IT?

QUITE HONESTLY, I CAN'T REALLY SAY. THIS ONE'S GOT ME BAFFLED. AS I TOLD MR. DOONESBURY...
ACTUALLY, I'M MR. DOONESBURY.

YOU ARE?
YES.

SO WHO'S THE GUY ON THE BEER RUN?
I THOUGHT HE WAS A FRIEND OF YOURS. SHOULD WE CALL SECURITY?

SO MANY WORDS UNSPOKEN...

...THANK GOODNESS.

YOU'RE A PIECE OF WORK, YOU KNOW THAT, J.J.?

IN A WAY, YOU LOST CONSCIOUS-NESS A LONG TIME AGO...

WAS IT MY FAULT? SOMETIMES I THINK SO. I TUNED YOU OUT SO OFTEN...

THERE WAS SO MUCH ABOUT YOU I DIDN'T GET. LIKE WHEN YOU GAVE BIRTH TO ALEX ON A CABLE SHOW—WHAT WAS **THAT** ABOUT? SOME DEEP NEED TO...TO...

J. J., IS THIS ANOTHER PIECE OF PERFORM-ANCE ART?
DRAT. NOT A WORD, OKAY?

I KNEW IT! I KNEW THIS WAS A PERFORMANCE!
NO, YOU DIDN'T.

YOU CALL THIS ART? GETTING PEOPLE TO BELIEVE YOU'RE DYING? WHAT IN GOD'S NAME WERE YOU THINKING?

YOU MAY NOT BE IN A COMA, J.J., BUT YOU'RE SICK, ALL RIGHT!
HE'S NOT TAKING THIS WELL.
GBTrudeau

SICK! DO YOU HEAR ME? SICK, SICK, SICK!
BETTER NOT MENTION THE MINI-CAM...

WHAT?
YOU HEARD ME—SHE'S FAKING IT!

WHAT ARE YOU TALKING ABOUT, MAN? LOOK AT HER!
IT'S ANOTHER PIECE OF PERFORMANCE ART! HER SICKEST YET!
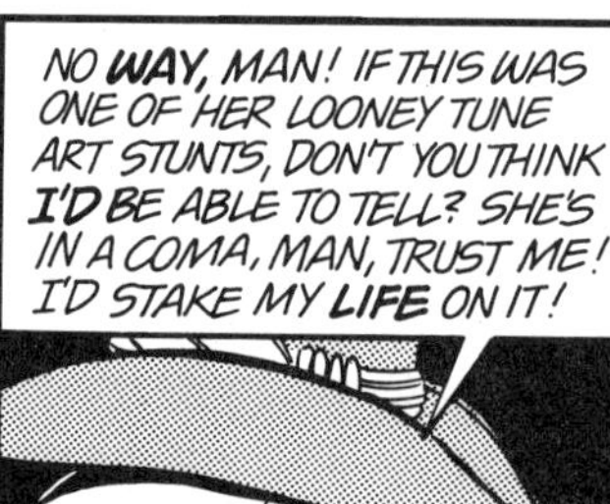
NO WAY, MAN! IF THIS WAS ONE OF HER LOONEY TUNE ART STUNTS, DON'T YOU THINK I'D BE ABLE TO TELL? SHE'S IN A COMA, MAN, TRUST ME! I'D STAKE MY LIFE ON IT!

FORGET IT, ZEKE—HE'S ON TO US.
US? ALL I DID WAS TURN ON THE CAMERA!
HAVE A NICE LIFE, YOU TWO.
GBTrudeau

I'LL SAY ONE THING FOR YOU, ZEKE...
WHAT'S THAT, MAN?

FOR THE PAST FEW MONTHS, I'VE BEEN THINKING IT WAS IMPOSSIBLE FOR YOU TWO TO SINK ANY LOWER. I SEE NOW JUST HOW WRONG I WAS!

APOLOGY ACCEPTED, MAN.
GBTrudeau

WAIT... WHAT WAS THAT AGAIN?
YOU JERK—WE GOT DISSED! AND YOU JUST STOOD THERE!

MICHAEL... PLEASE... WAIT! LET ME EXPLAIN!

EXPLAIN? J.J., HOW COULD YOU POSSIBLY EXPLAIN...
MIKE, IT WAS JUST SUPPOSED TO BE A BEAUTIFUL, LITTLE FILM ABOUT A COMA GIRL— ABOUT HOW PEOPLE REACT TO HER...

BUT IT WAS AN AWFUL THING TO DO TO YOU WITHOUT TELLING YOU. I SEE THAT NOW. I SWEAR I'LL MAKE IT UP TO YOU.

PLEASE, DON'T.
NO, NO, I WANT TO. SAY YOU'LL COME TO THE OPENING NIGHT PARTY.

MIKE, I'M SORRY I HURT YOU. IT WASN'T SUPPOSED TO TURN OUT THAT WAY...

I THOUGHT I WAS MAKING SOMETHING TRUTHFUL— A PIECE ABOUT PEOPLE CAUGHT IN THE ACT OF EXPRESSING THEIR REAL FEELINGS!

I KNOW WHAT YOU'RE THINKING—THAT I WAS BEING SELF-INVOLVED AND GRANDIOSE, THAT ALL I CARED ABOUT WERE MY OWN NEEDS. BUT I DON'T AGREE.

I WAS JUST BEING ME, THE WAY I AM.
DOING WHAT MAKES ME UNIQUE. SPECIAL.

I'M SO GLAD YOU'RE HOME, DAD-O-RAMA!
ME TOO, BABE. YOU GIVE UNCLE BERNIE ANY TROUBLE?

I WAS GOOD AS GOLD. HOW'S MOM?
SHE'S FINE. IT WASN'T SERIOUS. WE'LL SEND HER A CARD TOMORROW.

SHE WAS FAKING IT, WASN'T SHE?
YOUR MOTHER'S AN ARTIST, SWEETHEART. SHE GETS CONFUSED.

WELCOME BACK TO "ALL THINGS RECONSIDERED"! AS ALWAYS, I'M MARK SLACKMEYER, YOUR HOST...

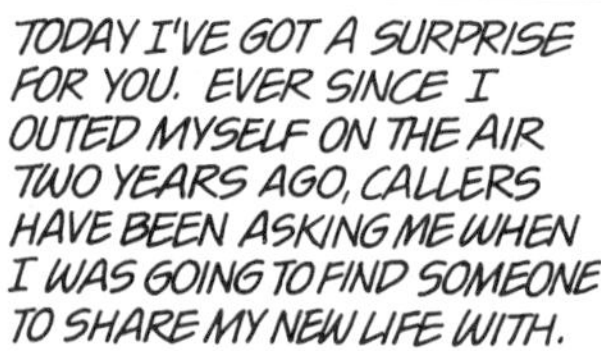
TODAY I'VE GOT A SURPRISE FOR YOU. EVER SINCE I OUTED MYSELF ON THE AIR TWO YEARS AGO, CALLERS HAVE BEEN ASKING ME WHEN I WAS GOING TO FIND SOMEONE TO SHARE MY NEW LIFE WITH.

WELL, IT FINALLY HAPPENED. HIS NAME IS NEIL, AND HE'S WITH US IN THE STUDIO TODAY. WELCOME, NEIL!

THANKS, MARK! HAPPY TO BE HERE!
SO TELL US ABOUT YOURSELF, GUY...

BY POPULAR DEMAND, WE'RE CHATTING TODAY WITH NEIL, MY SIGNIFICANT OTHER. WELCOME, NEIL.
THANKS, MARK!

NEIL, A LOT OF MY LISTENERS WERE BEGINNING TO WONDER IF I'D **EVER** GET INVOLVED WITH SOMEONE. TELL THEM A LITTLE ABOUT YOURSELF.

HAPPY TO, MARK. I'M A FORMER RHODES SCHOLAR, DOCTOR, LECTURER, AUTHOR, JOURNALIST, FILM MAKER AND ARTIST. IN MY SPARE TIME, I BUILD LOW-INCOME HOUSING AND WORK AN AIDS HOT-LINE.

HOW ABOUT **THAT,** GANG? DIDN'T I TELL YOU HE WAS A FIND?
ME? HEY, C'MON, MARK — **YOU'RE** THE CATCH!

I'M STILL CHATTING WITH MY NEW PERSON, NEIL...

NEIL, WHEN WE FIRST MET AT THAT EMBASSY PARTY, WHAT EXACTLY DID YOU SEE IN ME?

WELL, MARK, I GUESS I SAW A KIND OF TREMBLING VULNERABILITY. I SAW SOMEONE HONESTLY TRYING TO COME TO TERMS WITH WHO HE WAS. I WAS IMMEDIATELY INTRIGUED AND ATTRACTED.

SO YOU DIDN'T JUST SEE A FAMOUS SUPERSTAR RADIO PERSONALITY?
I DID, BUT IT DIDN'T MATTER. I DIDN'T CARE.

I'M MARK SLACK-MEYER, AND WE'RE STILL TALKING TO NEIL, MY SIGNIFI-CANT OTHER. IS THE CALLER THERE?

YEAH, MARK, I WAS JUST WONDERING HOW TWO PEOPLE LIKE YOU AND NEIL CONNECT IN THE AGE OF AIDS...

I MEAN, HOW DO YOU MAINTAIN A RELATION-SHIP WITH THE TERRIBLE SPECTER OF INFECTION HANG-ING OVER EVERYTHING?

ACTUALLY, WE GOT THAT COV-ERED, RIGHT, NEIL?
YOU MIGHT SAY THAT.
COOL. SO I DON'T HAVE TO WORRY ABOUT YOU GUYS?

YOU'RE ON THE AIR, CALLER!
YEAH, I HAVE A QUESTION FOR NEIL.

FIRE AWAY!
NEIL, ARE YOU AFRAID OF PEO-PLE FINDING OUT YOU'RE GAY?

THE REASON I ASK IS THAT YOU'RE OB-VIOUSLY TRYING TO DISGUISE YOUR VOICE. IT SOUNDS FORCED AND PHONY.

UM... NO, I JUST HAVE A COLD.
IT'S TRUE. HE LOOKS TERRIBLE.

GO AHEAD, CALLER!
YEAH, MARK, MY NAME'S BOB. I'M A LONG-TIME LISTENER...

I JUST WANT TO SAY IT TAKES A LOT OF GUTS GOING PUBLIC ON THE AIR LIKE YOU AND NEIL ARE DOING...

A LOT OF PEOPLE LIVE A LIE, KNOW WHAT I'M SAYING? THEY JUST SPEND THEIR WHOLE LIVES PRE-TENDING! YOU GUYS ARE DIFFERENT...

I'M HAPPY FOR YOU TWO, MAN.
THANKS, BOB.
YEAH, BOB, THANKS A LOT.

MIKE? IT'S BERNIE! WE NEED A **WEB SITE**!
WE DO?

YUP! WE'RE FALLING BEHIND. I WANT A STRONG WEB PRESENCE BY NEXT MONDAY, GOT IT?
UM... SURE. I'LL GET RIGHT ON IT, BERNIE. CONSIDER IT DONE.

BEEP! BEEP! BEEP!
GB Trudeau

ALEX? IT'S ME. WHAT'S A WEB SITE?
OH, DADDY, I'VE EXPLAINED IT TO YOU A **ZILLION** TIMES!

HANK, WHAT'S A WEB SITE?
IT'S AN INTERNET PRESENCE.

WHAT'S ON IT?
IT DOESN'T MATTER. BUILD IT AND THEY WILL COME.

WHY DO WE NEED ONE?
BECAUSE THE TECHNOLOGY EXISTS. ALSO, EVERYONE ELSE HAS ONE.
GB Trudeau

WHAT'S MY MOTIVATION?
FEAR. GREED. TAKE YOUR PICK.

HANK, HOW CAN I GET A WEB SITE UP AND RUNNING BY MONDAY? I'VE NEVER EVEN **SEEN** ONE BEFORE!
EASILY REMEDIED, MY MAN...

WE JUST CALL UP OUR NET SERVER — LIKE THAT — CLICK ON THE BROWSER, AND WE'RE IN!

THERE ARE OVER 100,000 SITES, BUT I'VE INDEXED SOME OF THE BEST ON A HOT LIST. THIS IS MY FAVORITE PAGE — THE DEMI MOORE TRACKING SYSTEM...

THE WHAT?
IT'S UPDATED EVERY HOUR. OH, WOW — SHE JUST HIT A WAITER!
GB Trudeau

OKAY, I'VE UPLOADED THE HOME PAGE GRAPHICS. NOW WHAT?
NOW YOU CAN ENTER YOUR TEXT.

"WELCOME TO BERNIE'S BYTE SHACK, THE HOTTEST NEW SITE ON THE WORLD WIDE WEB. WE HOPE YOU'LL ENJOY OUR..."

"...OUR..."

MY GOD... PEOPLE ARE ALREADY GATHERING! HUNDREDS OF 'EM!
THEY'RE WAITING FOR YOU TO FINISH THE SENTENCE.

LOOK AT THIS, HANK—WE'RE GETTING SCORES OF VISITORS EVEN WHILE I'M BUILDING THE SITE!

"WELCOME! HERE AT BERNIE'S BYTE SHACK, WE TAKE GREAT PRIDE IN OUR FINE LINE OF INFOTAINMENT SOFTWARE PRODUCTS..."
TAP! TAP!

"...ALL OF WHICH ARE AVAILABLE FOR PURCHASE RIGHT HERE!"
UH-OH...
TAP! TAP! TAP!

HEY... THEY'RE ALL LEAVING!
QUICK! OFFER THEM SOMETHING FREE!

WHAT'S THIS? AN ALL-NIGHTER? MIKE, YOU'RE BECOMING ONE OF US! ONE OF THE LITTLE PEOPLE!

SO HOW'S IT GOING? WHAT'D YOU UPLOAD?
WELL, BERNIE SAID HE WANTED THE SITE UP AND RUNNING BY TODAY.

ANYTHING I COULD THINK OF— PRODUCT SPECS, RELEASE DATES, PROMO COPY. BASICALLY I SCANNED IN EVERYTHING THAT WAS LYING AROUND THE OFFICE!

INCLUDING A CHINESE MENU!
IT WAS A LONG NIGHT. I'LL CLEAN IT UP TOMORROW.

WHAT TOWN IS THIS, DAD?
VEGAS, SON-MY OLD STOMPING GROUNDS!

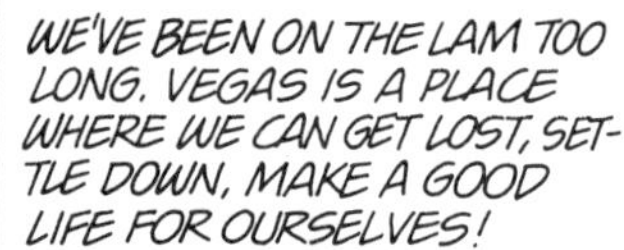
WE'VE BEEN ON THE LAM TOO LONG. VEGAS IS A PLACE WHERE WE CAN GET LOST, SETTLE DOWN, MAKE A GOOD LIFE FOR OURSELVES!

OH...

IS IT KID-FRIENDLY?
UM... I THINK SO. I'M PRETTY SURE THEY HAVE A SCHOOL SYSTEM.
GB Trudeau

DUKE AND SON ARE TOURING THE PEARL OF NEVADA.
WHAT CASINO IS THIS, DAD?
THE GOLDEN PIGEON. I USED TO WORK HERE...

I SHOULD BE ABLE TO GET ANOTHER GIG. I KNOW EVERYONE FROM THE C.E.O., STUCCO MORELL, RIGHT DOWN TO EDDY "THE FISH," WHO WORKS THE DOOR.

OKAY, NOW, LISTEN - I WANT YOU TO KEEP THE ENGINE IDLING, OKAY? AND THE WINDOW ROLLED DOWN. I MIGHT HAVE TO REGAIN ACCESS TO THE VEHICLE IN A HURRY.

THIS IS A JOB INTERVIEW?
IT'S BEEN AWHILE. I CAN'T RECALL WHETHER I OWE ANYBODY MONEY.
GB Trudeau

HEY, PAL! IS MR. MEYER IN TONIGHT?
NO, HE'S OUT OF TOWN. WE DON'T EXPECT HIM BACK FOR 7 TO 10 YEARS.

MR. MORELL AROUND, KID?
NO, SIR. NOT SINCE SOMEONE PLANTED THAT ICE PICK IN HIS FOREHEAD.

SEEN EDDY "THE FISH" LATELY?
LAST TIME I SEEN FISH, THEY WAS PULLIN' HIM OUTA A CEMENT MIXER.

FIND ANY OF YOUR OLD BUDS, DAD?
NAH, THERE'S BEEN A TURNOVER.
GB Trudeau

HEY... TONY "THE PICK"! IS THAT YOU?
DUKE! WELL, I'LL BE DAMNED! LONG TIME, MAN!

YEAH, TOO LONG. I DON'T KNOW ANYONE AROUND HERE ANYMORE...
YEAH, THE NEW GENERATION! BUNCH OF BEAN-COUNTERS...

WELL, IT'S GOOD TO BE BACK. I DON'T KNOW WHY I EVER LEFT...
YOU LEFT BECAUSE YOU STOLE FROM THE HOUSE SKIM, AND CHICAGO PUT OUT A HIT ON YOU.
GB Trudeau

OH... RIGHT. WE CAN LAUGH ABOUT THAT NOW, THOUGH, RIGHT?
I DON'T KNOW. I'M GOING TO HAVE TO CHECK.

HEY, DAD—LOOK! SHOWGIRLS!
WHAT HAPPENED TO THIS TOWN, TONY? I BARELY RECOGNIZE IT ANYMORE!

A LOT OF NEW PLAYERS, DUKE. AND THEY DO THINGS DIFFERENTLY THAN THE OLD OUTFIT...

WE GOT NEW MANAGEMENT HERE, AND THEY RUN THE JOINT MUCH MORE LIKE A BUSINESS. THESE GUYS ARE REALLY COLD—TOTALLY RUTHLESS!
GB Trudeau

NOT THE PHILLY MOB?
NO, NO, TIME-WARNER.

EARL, LET ME ASK YOU SOMETHING. WHEN YOU THINK OF LAS VEGAS, WHAT COMES TO MIND?

LOTS OF COOL STUFF—LIKE THE PYRAMID RIDES, THE EXPLODING VOLCANO, THE AS1 SIM THEATER, WET 'N WILD, GRAND SCAM, YOU NAME IT!
ANYTHING ELSE?

UM... LIKE WHAT?
LIKE WHAT? EVER HEARD OF GAMBLING? PROSTITUTION? HELLO?
GB Trudeau

OH, YOU MEAN THE PARENT STUFF! SURE, DAD!
DAMN, I HATE CHANGE...

SON, VOLCANO ERUPTIONS AND TALKING CAESAR STATUES ARE ALL VERY FINE, BUT **THIS** IS WHERE THE REAL MAGIC HAPPENS- THE **CA-SINO!**

THERE ARE OVER 100 MILLION GAMBLERS IN THIS COUNTRY, INCLUDING 4 MILLION PROB-LEM GAMBLERS, 40,000 HIGH ROLLERS, AND COUNTLESS PROFESSIONAL CHEATS...

THE CASINOS IN THIS TOWN CLEAR **SIX BILLION** DOLLARS A YEAR! THAT'S $200 PRO-FIT A SECOND! **MORE** THAN ENOUGH FOR EVERYONE!
GBTrudeau

INCLUD-ING THE CHEATERS?
I'M GET-TING TO THAT...

REMEMBER, EARL, ON SLOTS, THE HIGHER THE BET, THE LOOSER THE **MACHINE**. HOUSE TAKE IS ONLY 5% ON DOLLAR SLOTS.

BUT CRAPS ARE BETTER- THE VIG IS ONLY .6%! WITH ROULETTE, YOU GOT A HOUSE ADVANTAGE OF 5.26%.
SO STAY AWAY FROM WHEELS- THEY'RE ALL SUCKER GAMES.

WOW, DAD...
WOW WHAT, KID?
GBTrudeau

I DUNNO. SOMETIMES YOU SEEM TEN FEET TALL TO ME...
WELL, I'M IN MY ELE-MENT HERE.

DAD, THERE'S **GOT** TO BE A WAY TO BEAT THE HOUSE, RIGHT?
EARL, LET ME TELL YOU A STORY...

MANY YEARS AGO, SOMEONE YOU KNOW **CAME** TO THIS TOWN WITH HIS LIFE SAVINGS, A "SYSTEM" AND AN ATTITUDE. HE CHECKED INTO THE GOLDEN PIGEON, AND TWO HOURS LATER, ALL HE HAD LEFT WAS THE ATTITUDE.

GBTrudeau

SO WHAT'S THE MORAL OF THAT LITTLE STORY?
UM... THERE'S A MORAL?

THINK, KID!
HOW SHOULD **I** KNOW? NONE OF YOUR STOR-IES EVER HAD A MORAL BE-FORE!

KNOW WHAT YOU'D LIKE TO FIND UNDER THE TREE THIS YEAR, BABE?
UH-HUH!

I WANT A PACKARD BELL WITH A 133 MHz PROCESSOR IN A MULTIMEDIA MINITOWER WITH A 2.1 GIGABYTE HARD DRIVE! HINT, HINT, SANTA!

UM... HONEY, THAT'S A LOT OF COMPUTER...
I KNOW, POPPY.
GB Trudeau

ARE YOU SURE YOU'RE READY FOR...
POPPY, ALL THE KIDS IN SEATTLE HAVE MUSCLE MA-CHINES! I'M LIKE THE LAST TO GO PENTIUM!

OKAY, LET ME GET THIS DOWN. FOR CHRISTMAS YOU WANT A NEW PC...
UH-HUH...

BUT IT'S GOT TO HAVE A PENTIUM PROCESSOR OF 133 MHz OR BETTER! ANYTHING LESS AND I'LL LOSE FACE AT SCHOOL!

YOU WILL?
AND FOR STOCKING STUFFERS, I WANT A 8MB 72-PIN SIMM, A 28.8 MODEM, AND A PERI-PHERAL INTER-FACE CABLE.
GB Trudeau

STOCKING STUFFERS?
DADS, CAN I GET MY EARS PIERCED FOR CHRISTMAS?

ANYTHING ELSE YOU WANT FOR CHRISTMAS, BABE?
YES, INDEED, POPSICLE! I WANT NEAT BATH STUFF! SOAP, FOAMING LOTION...

YOU DO? ISN'T THAT A LITTLE FAIRY PRIN-CESSY FOR YOU?
WHAT DO YOU MEAN BY THAT?

EXCUSE ME, DADDY, BUT WHAT'S WRONG WITH WANT-ING TO SMELL LIKE A FAIRY PRINCESS? YOU HAVE A PROBLEM WITH THAT? SO SUE ME!
GB Trudeau

OKAY, OKAY, WHAT BRAND DO FAIRY PRINCESSES USE?
THE BODY SHOP. ASK FOR SAVE-THE-MANATEE BATH BEADS.

YOU'RE TURNING INTO QUITE THE LITTLE PROPELLER-HEAD, AREN'T YOU, ALEX?
TAP! TAP!

UH-HUH. MY TEACHER SAYS I'M MORE COMPUTER-LITERATE THAN ANYONE IN MY CLASS, EVEN THOUGH MOST OF THE KIDS HAVE LIVED IN SEATTLE THEIR WHOLE LIVES!
WOW...

YOU KNOW WHAT, DADDY?
WHAT'S THAT, BABE?

I DON'T FEEL LIKE A TINY SPECK OF DIRT ANYMORE.
WELL, I NEVER COULD SEE THAT MYSELF.

YOU KNOW WHAT WE OUGHT TO SEND MOMMY FOR CHRISTMAS, DAD?
WHAT'S THAT, HONEY?

I SAW THIS NEAT KEY CHAIN WITH A LITTLE FOUR-LEAF CLOVER. I FIGURE MOMMY COULD USE A LITTLE LUCK!
GOOD IDEA, SWEETHEART.

DON'T WORRY, DADDY- I'LL PAY FOR IT.
NO, NO, I'LL CHIP IN...

MOMSTER?
HI, LITTLE GIRL! BEEN HAVING A NICE CHRISTMAS?

UH-HUH. HEY, GUESS WHAT, MOMMY! WE SENT YOU A PRESENT TODAY!
YOU DID?

YUP! I PICKED IT OUT BY MYSELF! I DIDN'T LET DADDY HELP AT ALL!
WHY NOT, SWEETHEART?

MOMMY, DAD WOULD HAVE SENT YOU A BUCKET OF BOOGERS!
ALEX!
WELL, I CAN UNDERSTAND THAT, HONEY.

CHRISTMAS MORNING AT THE DOONESBURY HOUSE...

...THE SMELL OF THE COFFEE, THE SOUND OF BING CROSBY...
I'M DREAMING OF A WHIIITE...

...THE CRACKLING FIRE...

...THE CRIES OF INGRATITUDE.
DADDY! IT HAS NO EXTERNAL RAM CACHE!
YOU'RE WELCOME.

ALEX! THIS IS GREAT! I'VE ALWAYS WANTED ONE! DID YOU MAKE IT?

UH-HUH. AS A CLASS PROJECT. YOU REALLY LIKE IT, POPSTER?
LIKE IT? I LOVE IT!

IN FACT, I LOVE IT SO MUCH, I'M GOING TO CALL YOUR TEACHER TO THANK HER FOR ASSIGNING IT!

WHAT IS IT?
A BOOK-MARK.

SO DID BENJY MAKE IT HOME, MA?
YES. BOTH HE AND HENRY. JUST IN TIME FOR CHRISTMAS DINNER.
DING-DONG!

HEY, ALEX! COULD YOU GET THE DOOR? I'M TALKING WITH GRANNY!
SO HOW HAS YOUR DAY GONE, DEAR?

WELL, IT STARTED OUT A LITTLE SHAKY — I GOT ALEX THE WRONG COMPUTER—BUT OTHER THAN THAT, GREAT! IN FACT, THIS MAY BE THE HAPPIEST CHRISTMAS I'VE HAD IN YEARS!

MOMMY!
OF COURSE, IT'S NOT OVER YET...

MOMMY!
MERRY CHRISTMAS, LITTLE ONE.

WHAT ARE YOU DOING HERE?
WHAT DO YOU MEAN? IT'S CHRISTMAS! I THOUGHT MAYBE WE COULD GO TO LUNCH! WOULD YOU LIKE THAT?

MY GOODNESS, JUST LOOK AT YOU! HAVE YOU BEEN GROWING ON ME AGAIN? BOY, I MISSED YOU! DID YOU MISS ME, SWEETHEART?

IS THAT THE SLEAZEBAG? IN THE PICK-UP?
YOUR UNCLE ZEKE? WHY, YES!
ZEKE! WAVE!

J.J.— WHAT A SURPRISE...
WELL, I WAS IN THE NEIGHBORHOOD!

NEIGHBORHOOD? WHAT NEIGHBORHOOD? THE AMERICAN WEST?
WOULD IT BE OKAY IF I TOOK HER OUT TO LUNCH?

YEAH, I SUPPOSE...
WHAT? I DON'T WANT TO HAVE LUNCH WITH HER AND HER STUPID BOYFRIEND!
COME ON, HONEY...

GOOD LUCK.
THANKS FOR POISONING HER AGAINST ME, MIKE.
DADDY'S DATING, TOO, YOU KNOW! HE'S PRACTICALLY MARRIED!

WHERE DO YOU WANT TO GO FOR LUNCH, ALEX? HO JO'S OKAY?
I DON'T CARE. HE'S NOT COMING, IS HE?

OF COURSE HE IS! HONEY, I'D LIKE YOU TO MEET ZEKE! ZEKE, THIS IS ALEX!

HOW YOU DOING, KID?
I WAS DOING GREAT UNTIL ABOUT FIVE MINUTES AGO, MR. SLEAZEBAG!

PLEASE CALL ME ZEKE.
GOSH, I THINK NOT, MR. SLEAZEBAG!

AFTER LUNCH, I THOUGHT WE'D GO TO THE MALL, OKAY, LITTLE GIRL?

UM... THAT'S SORT OF A BORING IDEA, MOMMY...
EVEN IF WE GOT YOUR EARS PIERCED?

WHAT? YOU **MEAN** IT, MOMMY?
I DON'T SEE WHY NOT. YOU'RE ALREADY A BIG SIX-YEAR-OLD!

SEVEN.
SEVEN. I KNEW THAT.
ME, TOO.
GBTrudeau

BE RIGHT BACK. I'M GOING TO CALL THE MALL TO SEE IF THEY CAN DO ALEX'S EARS...
HOLD IT. WHAT DO I TALK TO HER ABOUT?

JUST STAY ON FUN STUFF — YOU KNOW, ROCK MUSIC OR MOVIES...

GBTrudeau

SO, KID — SEEN "SHOWGIRLS" YET?
GOSH, NOT YET, MR. SCUZZBALL!

LOOK, KID, I KNOW WHERE YOU'RE COMIN' FROM HERE...

HELL, I HAD **FOUR** STEPFATHERS AND I HATED **ALL** OF THEM! BUT WE MANAGED.

IF YOU'LL JUST TAKE THE TIME TO GET TO KNOW ME, I...
GOSH, WHAT FOR, MR. SLEAZE-O-MATIC? I ALREADY KNOW YOU'RE A CREEP!

HEY, **SIT** ON IT, YOU LITTLE TWERP!
MOM! **HELP!** UNCLE ZEKE IS BEING VERBALLY ABUSIVE!
GBTrudeau

NOW, KEEP THOSE BAND-AIDS ON YOUR EARS UNTIL DADDY SAYS IT'S OKAY TO TAKE THEM OFF, OKAY, ALEX? WE DON'T WANT THEM TO GET INFECTED...
OKAY, MOMMY.

FUN DAY, WASN'T IT, BABY?
IT WOULD HAVE BEEN FUNNER WITHOUT A CERTAIN NOBODY.
THE FEEL-ING'S MUTUAL, KID...

YOU REMIND ME OF WHY I NEVER WANTED KIDS OF MY OWN!

CAREFUL, ZEKE...
YEAH, DODO-HEAD, SHE'S A MOTHER! DON'T MAKE HER CHOOSE BETWEEN US!

I'M HOME, POPMEISTER!
HOW'D IT GO, BABE?

OKAY, I GUESS. IT WOULD'VE BEEN BETTER WITHOUT THE JERKHEAD.
ALEX, WHY DO YOU HAVE BAND-AIDS ON YOUR EARS?

UM... I GOT MY EARS PIERCED. MOM TOOK ME TO THE MALL.
ALEX, YOU'RE ONLY SEVEN! I TOLD YOU YOU'D HAVE TO WAIT UN-TIL YOU WERE AT LEAST 13!

POPPY, MOM WAS REACHING OUT.
WITH A NEEDLE?

POPPY, DON'T YOU THINK OL' MOMSTER HAS MADE A BIG MESS OF HER LIFE?
SWEETER, EVEN IF I THOUGHT SO, I'D NEVER TELL YOU.

WHY NOT?
BECAUSE DIVORCE IS ROUGH ENOUGH ON A KID WITHOUT PAR-ENTS TEARING EACH OTHER DOWN.

WOW... THAT'S PRETTY BIG OF YOU, DADDY...

I DON'T HAVE TO BE THAT BIG, DO I?
HECK, NO, YOU'RE THE VICTIM. GO NUTS.

THIS IS ROLAND HEDLEY. EVER NOTICE THAT THE WORD "ENVIRONMENT" DOESN'T EVEN APPEAR **ONCE** IN THE 167-PAGE "CONTRACT WITH AMERICA"?
CONTRACT WITH AMERICA

THAT'S BECAUSE FOCUS GROUPS TOLD ITS AUTHORS THEY **CARE** ABOUT THEIR COUNTRY'S NATURAL ASSETS AND WANT TO SEE THEM PROTECTED, NOT EXPLOITED.

TOO BAD, AMERICA! IN THE NAME OF "JOB ENHANCEMENT," THE G.O.P. IS NOW IN THE PROCESS OF LIQUIDATING **YOUR** NATIONAL RESOURCES! LET'S TAKE A PEEK...

LOT #13! TONGASS NATIONAL **FOREST!**
DO I HEAR PENNIES A TREE?
LOT #13

THE G.O.P. LIQUIDATION AUCTION OF OUR NATIONAL ASSETS.
ON THE BLOCK, LOT #13— OLD-GROWTH **TREES** FROM TONGASS NATIONAL FOREST!
30
75

$1.45 A TREE!
#1.45 A TREE! GOING ONCE, GOING TWICE...

C'MON, FOLKS, THESE ARE 500-YEAR-OLD TREES! THINK OF THE **JOBS** THESE SUCKERS WILL CREATE!

$1.46!
SOLD!
NOW **THAT'S** DEFICIT REDUCTION!
BAM!

LOT #271! 22 MILLION ACRES OF RESOURCE-RICH **UTAH WILDERNESS!** WHAT AM I BID?
LOT #271

THE EXTRACTION INDUSTRIES BID A **PITTANCE!**
THE BID IS A PITTANCE! GOING ONCE, GOING TWICE...
113

C'MON, FOLKS, THESE ASSETS ARE WORTH **BILLIONS!** LET'S NOT DISAPPOINT MY COLLEAGUES FROM UTAH...

DID I MENTION THE GENEROUS FINDER'S FEE?
SAY NO MORE!
SOLD!
BAM!

NEXT UP—**GRAZING RIGHTS!** VALUED AT $10 A MONTH PER ACRE, I'D LIKE TO OPEN THE BIDDING AT ONE-**TENTH** OF THAT!

DO I HEAR A BID OF $1?
RIGHT HERE, MR. SPEAKER! ME AND THE BOYS'LL SEE YOU AT EIGHT BITS!
72

EIGHT BITS FROM THE CORPORATE COWBOYS! GOING ONCE, GOING TWICE...
...PROVIDED THE TAXPAYERS PONY UP $500 MILLION TO MAINTAIN THE LAND!

SOLD!
PROVIDED **YOU** AGREE TO OVER-GRAZE!
HELL, YES! GOT OUR WORD ON IT!

SOLD! DESPOILING RIGHTS TO THE **ARCTIC WILDLIFE REFUGE** GO TO MR. JIM ANDREWS OF UNIVERSAL PETROLEUM!
BAM!

THANKS FOR CONTRI-BUTING TO AMERICA'S ENERGY SECURITY, MR. AN-DREWS!
ACTUALLY, WE'LL BE SENDING THE OIL TO ITS NAT-URAL MARKET—JAPAN. IT'S A LOT CHEAPER TO SHIP IT TO ASIA.
73

OH.

WELL, I'M SURE A GRATE-FUL JAPAN SALUTES YOU, SIR!
YEAH, I FEEL GOOD ABOUT THAT.

QUESTION FROM THE FLOOR?
YES, I'M A BUSI-NESSMAN...

20 YEARS AGO, THE FOLKS AT E.P.A. SHOWED ME THAT BY MANAGING RESOURCES WISELY, OUR COMPANY COULD IN FACT FLOURISH, DOING WELL AND GOOD AT THE SAME TIME...

IT TOOK US A WHILE TO GET IT RIGHT, BUT TODAY WE TAKE PRIDE IN BEING GOOD CORPOR-ATE CITIZENS. WHY ARE YOU TRY-ING TO ROLL BACK EVERYTHING POSITIVE THAT BUSINESS AND GOVERNMENT HAVE ACCOMP-LISHED IN PARTNERSHIP?

I TAKE IT YOU'RE FROM BEN AND JERRY'S...
NO, A POWER COMPANY. COULD YOU AN-SWER THE QUESTION?

GOOD MORNING. I'D LIKE TO WELCOME EVERYONE TO THE CYBERCITIZENS-FOR-STEVE-FORBES ORGANIZATIONAL MEETING!

AS YOU KNOW, AT THE CORE OF EVERY GREAT CAMPAIGN ARE THE VOLUNTEERS WHO BELIEVE, WHO SHARE THE DREAM!

I SHARE THE FORBES DREAM OF A FLAT TAX! I BELIEVE! WHO ELSE HERE SHARES THE DREAM? WHO BELIEVES?

YEAH... OVER HERE.
I MIGHT BE GETTING TOO OLD FOR THIS...
EVE
BES
IN '96

CYBERCITIZENS-FOR-STEVE-FORBES HAVE GATHERED AT BERNIE'S BYTE SHACK.
LET'S BE CLEAR WHAT'S AT STAKE, MY FRIENDS...

MOST OF US HERE ARE LOADED UP WITH STOCK OPTIONS! AND WE DESERVE 'EM—WE BUILT THIS INDUSTRY, BUT WHAT'S THE POINT IF WE LOSE IT ALL IN TAXES?

THAT'S WHY THE FORBES CAMPAIGN IS A HOLY CRUSADE! THAT'S WHY WE MUST FIGHT WITH EVERY FIBER IN OUR...
BOB?

WHAT?
COULD WE TAKE A BREAK? I WANT TO CHECK MY E-MAIL.
STEVE FORBES
IDENT IN '96

HEY... WHAT'S GOING ON IN HERE?

UM... IT'S A MEETING FOR STEVE FORBES VOLUNTEERS.
OH, YEAH? NOT MUCH OF A TURN-OUT.

I KNOW. I ALWAYS SEEM TO BE ATTRACTED TO LOST CAUSES.
WELL, WHAT'S THE POINT OF GETTING INVOLVED IN A CAMPAIGN ANYWAY, YOU KNOW?

TO MEET GIRLS.
TO GIVE SOMETHING BACK.
AS IF! I HAVEN'T GOTTEN ANYTHING YET!

I'M KIM ROSENTHAL, BY THE WAY. I'M IN CODING.
MIKE DOONES-BURY. MARKETING.

OH, RIGHT. I THOUGHT I RECOGNIZED YOU FROM ONE OF THE LAUNCH MEETINGS. YOU BEEN ON TEAM BERNIE LONG?
LESS THAN A YEAR. HOW ABOUT YOU?

TWO YEARS... EVER SINCE I BLEW OFF MY COMP SCI Ph.D. AT M.I.T....
M.I.T. WAS TOO MUCH?

AS IF. TOTALLY TOO EASY.
OH... SURE. I'VE HEARD THAT.

SO YOU LIKE THIS FORBES PERSON, HUH?
YEAH, ESPECIAL-LY ON CAPITAL GAINS. IT HELPS THAT I'M AN EQUITY PLAYER HERE.

ME, TOO. LET ME SEE HIS PROGRAM...
SHE'S HUMOR-ING ME...
SURE!

HMM... NO TAX WHEN WE CASH OUT— I LIKE IT!
GOD... I WONDER IF SHE'D EVER GO OUT WITH ME...

BOOT ME UP, YOU JERK!
IN YOUR DREAMS, MIKE...

BERNIE, I MET A VERY COOL LADY AT THE FORBES MEETING LAST NIGHT. SHE'S ONE OF YOUR CODERS.

MIKE, IF SHE WORKS FOR ME, SHE'S TOO YOUNG FOR YOU. TELL ME WHAT YOU LIKE ABOUT FORBES.

UM... WELL, YOU KNOW ABOUT THE FLAT TAX. ASIDE FROM THAT, I GUESS I LIKE HIS OVERALL APPROACH TO DOWN-SIZING THE GOVERNMENT.

ALSO, HE'S A RICH GEEK WITH GLASSES AND BAD HAIR.
ONE OF US? SIGN ME UP.

KNOCK, KNOCK. KIM?
HI, MIKE. COME ON IN...

UM... WHERE ARE YOU?
DOWN HERE. PICKING UP MY DINNER.

I JUST DUMPED A WHOLE-DAMN BAG OF SKITTLES ON THE FLOOR!

SKITTLES ARE YOUR DINNER?
I DON'T HAVE **TIME** FOR THIS!
MIKE, I'LL GIVE YOU HALF OF ANY YOU FIND...

SKITTLES ARE YOUR DINNER?
YEAH, AND I JUST DUMPED THEM ALL OVER THE FLOOR...

HERE, LET ME HELP, KIM...
THANKS.
HEY, YOU.

WHAT?
YOU'RE STILL CUTE.

UM... IT'S THE LIGHT. FROM THE SURGE PROTECTOR.
OH.
DO YOU THINK THESE ARE TOO DIRTY TO EAT?

YOU REALLY LIKE SKITTLES?
ARE YOU KIDDING? THEY TOTALLY **RULE** THEIR FOOD GROUP!

MY FAVORITE FUEL, THOUGH, IS NACHOS. DID YOU KNOW YOU CAN MELT A JAR OF VELVEETA CHEESE SPREAD WITH A DESK LAMP?

YOU JUST POUR IT ON THE CHIPS, SPRINKLE ON SOME PEPPERS, CRACK OPEN A DIET DR. PEPPER — ET **VOILÀ**!

DINNER?
NO, NO, BREAKFAST. YOU REALLY **ARE** FROM ANOTHER TRIBE, AREN'T YOU?

SO WHATCHA DOING IN THE CODE BUILDING, MIKE? CANVASSING?

NO, NO, I JUST SAW YOUR LIGHT ON, AND WONDERED WHY YOU WERE HERE SO LATE...
GOT A BIG SHIP DATE TO MEET. WE'VE ALL BEEN CAMPING OUT.

WELL, THAT WOULD EXPLAIN THE HACKER'S DIET...
HEY, YOU KNOW SOMETHING, MIKE? WE LIKE EACH OTHER.
©B Trudeau

WE DO?
THAT'S THE BUZZ. I'VE JUST BEEN TOO BUSY TO FOLLOW UP.

LISTEN, MIKE, I KNOW IT'S 3:00 A.M. AND YOU'RE PROBABLY BUSY, BUT YOU WANT TO GO OUT AND GET SOME COFFEE?

UH... SURE. YOU DON'T SUPPOSE THE COMPANY HAS ANY RULE AGAINST FRATERNIZATION, DO YOU?
IF IT DOES, HALF THE PEOPLE I KNOW HAVE BROKEN IT!

WELL, MAYBE I SHOULD CHECK... YOU KNOW, JUST TO BE ON THE SAFE SIDE...

THIS BETTER BE IMPORTANT.
OH.
NEVER MIND.
©B Trudeau

MIND IF I SWING BY MY HOUSE, MIKE? I GOTTA FEED MY CAT...

FINE.
YOU CAN MEET MY HOUSEMATES. MOST OF 'EM ARE STILL UP AT THIS HOUR.

HOUSEMATES? YOU MEAN, OTHER PEOPLE IN THEIR 20s?
UH-HUH. IS THIS A PROBLEM?

THEY'LL ALL BE SPEAKING IN GENERATIONAL CODE. I'LL APPEAR CLUELESS.
GOOD POINT. BETTER WAIT IN THE CAR.
©B Trudeau

OKAY... OKAY... I GUESS... OKAY...

OKAY... OKAY... FINE.

OKAY...OKAY... GOOD, I GUESS... FINE...OKAY.

OKAY, I GUESS... UH-HUH...UH-HUH... FINE...FINE... OKAY...BYE.

HOW'S MOMMY, ALEX?
WHO CARES?

WELL, I CARE. AND SO DO YOU, BABE.
WHY? MOMMY DOESN'T CARE ABOUT **ME**!

SURE SHE DOES...
DADDY, IF MOMMY **REALLY** LOVED ME, SHE'D **FIGHT** FOR ME! SHE'D TRY TO TAKE ME IN AN UGLY **CUSTODY BATTLE**!

SHE WOULD?
SHE'D HIRE **JOHNNIE COCHRAN**! WE'D HAVE TO FLEE TO **MEXICO**! OR **MICHIGAN**! SOME-PLACE LIKE THAT!

MAN... I HAVE A WHOLE NEW RESPECT FOR GUMSHOES...

THIS IS HARD **WORK**!

THE FURTHER ADVENTURES OF O.J., P.I.
SORRY I CAN'T HELP, JUICE...

YOU'RE SURE NEITHER YOU NOR ANY FAMILY MEMBER HAD A GRUDGE AGAINST MY WIFE?
YES, I'M SURE.

DARN! ANOTHER DEAD END!
YOU KNOW, JUICE, YOU MIGHT BE GOING ABOUT YOUR INVESTIGATION THE WRONG WAY.

WHAT DO YOU MEAN?
WELL, YOU SAY YOU'RE LOOKING FOR YOUR WIFE'S KILLER, BUT WHAT ABOUT THE GOLDMAN BOY ~ HE WAS KILLED, TOO! MAYBE **HE** WAS THE TARGET, AND **NICOLE** WAS THE INNOCENT BYSTANDER!

HEY... YOU KNOW, I NEVER THOUGHT OF THAT...

THINK I SHOULD BE CHARGING THE GOLDMANS FOR THEIR SHARE OF THE INVESTIGATION?
MIGHT AS WELL. I HEAR THEY'LL BE COMING INTO A LOT OF MONEY ONE DAY.

HOW MANY UNITS ARE WE SHIPPING? 35,000? UH-HUH...

OKAY, I'LL WANT TO CHECK EACH CARTON MYSELF.

...AND WE EXPECT TO SHIP AROUND FEBRUARY 19...
OKAY, BUT I WANT TO COPYREAD ALL THE SPEC BOOKS — AND THE REVISIONS.

BERNIE, YOU CAN'T REVIEW ALL THAT MINUTIA — YOU'RE CEO OF A $400 MILLION SOFTWARE CONCERN!
SO?

SO WE NEED YOU TO PROVIDE THE BIG PICTURE. YOU'RE NOT OPERATING OUT OF YOUR GAR-AGE ANYMORE!

IF YOU MICRO-MANAGE EVERY-THING, YOU'LL...
BRRING!
HOLD THAT THOUGHT, WILL YOU, MIKE?

BERNIE'S BYTE SHACK, HOW MAY I DIRECT YOUR CALL?

SEE?
WHAT?
YEAH, I'D LIKE TO ORDER A MOUSE PAD.

ANY SIGN OF HIM?
NONE!

DID YOU CHECK THE HARD DRIVE?
FIRST PLACE I LOOKED.

Edit View Special
UM... HI, FOLKS. WE HAVE SOMETHING A LITTLE UNSETTLING TO REPORT.

Special
AS MANY OF YOU KNOW, THIS FINE FEATURE WAS RECENTLY TRANSFERRED TO ELECTRONIC FILE...
...WHICH SUBSTANTIALLY FACILITATES ITS DISTRIBUTION TO YOU, THE VALUED READER!

UNFORTUNATELY, IN ALL THE CONFUSION, ONE OF THE CHARACTER FILES GOT LOST...
ZONKER'S!

THAT'S RIGHT — WE NO LONGER HAVE **ANY** RECORD OF ZONKER AT ALL — NO SKETCHES, NO MODEL SHEETS, NO BACK-UP FILES! IT'S AS IF HE NEVER **EXISTED!** THE LOSS TO THIS FRANCHISE IS INCALCULABLE...

GUYS! I **FOUND** HIM!
HUH?...
HEELP!
GBTrudeau

File Edit View Special
WHAT ARE YOU **DOING** IN THERE, ZONKER?
LOOKING FOR LOOSE CHANGE! GET ME **OUT!**
NEVER MIND — SEE YOU NEXT WEEK!
Trash

AHEM.

WHAT IS IT, MY GOOD MAN? DO YOU HAVE A CATCH IN YOUR THROAT? DO YOU HAVE A COLD? DO YOU NEED A DOCTOR? OUT WITH IT!

GOODNESS! TWO TITMICE ON THE SAME OUTING?
IT MADE THE AUDUBON NEWS! DID I EVER TELL YOU THAT STORY?

MAYBE YOU SHOULD SAVE IT, JEREMY DEAR. I THINK THE RESTAURANT STAFF WOULD LIKE TO GO HOME...
YOU'RE RIGHT AS USUAL! I'LL ASK THE GARÇON TO PREPARE OUR BILL.

BEFORE I DO, THOUGH, LET ME ASK YOU SOMETHING, MRS. D. IS IT JUST ME OR WAS THIS EVENING A BIG SUCCESS—TOP TO BOTTOM, SOUP TO NUTS?

IT'S GONE SWIMMINGLY, DEAR. NONE OF THE LITTLE UPSETS WE'VE HAD IN THE PAST.
REALLY? YOU TRULY MEAN IT?

OF COURSE I DO, DEAR...
GADZOOKS! IF I'D KNOWN IT WOULD GO THIS WELL, I **NEVER** WOULD HAVE FORGOTTEN MY WALLET!

YOU FORGOT YOUR WALLET?
CAN YOU BELIEVE IT? WE'LL BE LAUGHING ABOUT THIS ONE FOR **YEARS** TO COME!

HEY... ANOTHER HIT ON MY WEB PAGE!

I WONDER WHAT SHE LOOKS LIKE...

WHATCHA DOIN', POP-O-RAMA?

I'M UPDATING MY WEB SITE, SWEETHEART. IT'S KIND OF A TIP SHEET ON SOFTWARE MARKETING TRENDS...

I THINK IT'S BEGINNING TO CATCH ON. ALMOST 100 PEOPLE HAVE LOGGED ON SO FAR.
NEATO! NOW WE **BOTH** HAVE WEB PAGES!

YOU HAVE A WEB PAGE?
UH-HUH. MY COMPUTER TEACHER SHOWED US HOW TO MAKE 'EM. MINE'S ABOUT COOL GAMES AND STUFF. I KINDA' REVIEW 'EM.

SOUNDS LIKE FUN, SQUIRT! HAD ANY VISITORS YET?
UH-HUH. LAST WEEK I HAD 156,000 HITS.

GOOD LUCK, POPSTER! DON'T FORGET TO USE COLOR!
KIDS! VISIT THE DOONESBURY ELECTRONIC TOWN HALL AT http://www.doonesbury.com

I DON'T GET IT... I **NEVER** GET IT!

MAYBE I'M IRONY-CHALLENGED...

HMM... WONDER WHAT HE'S TRYING TO SAY HERE... IT'S NOT TERRIBLY CLEAR...

HEY, READER! IS THIS YOU? DO YOU SOMETIMES SCRATCH **YOUR** HEAD OVER ONE OF OUR INSTALLMENTS?
IF SO, THEN CALL THE DOONESBURY **TECHNICAL SUPPORT HOTLINE!**

OUR TRAINED FACILITATORS ARE STANDING BY TO HELP YOU MAKE SENSE OF OUR FINE, CHARACTER-DRIVEN HUMOR!
IN PANEL THREE, B.D. DOESN'T KNOW WHAT'S UP...
AND THE BOMB IS AN ICON! GET IT?

IF IT'S CONTEXT YOU NEED, WE'LL EXPLAIN THE CURRENT EVENT THAT INSPIRED THE STRIP—AND REFERENCE IT FOR YOU SO YOU CAN FIND OUT MORE!
TIME

IF, AFTER ALL THAT, YOU **STILL** DON'T GET THE JOKE—OR YOU GET IT, BUT THINK IT'S LAME...
WE'LL SEND YOU A **BRAND-NEW** STRIP—AT **OUR** EXPENSE!

WHY? BECAUSE WE **VALUE** YOUR PATRONAGE! SO CALL NOW AT 1-800...
YOU **MORON!** I JUST **EXPLAINED** THAT! HELLOOO? ANYONE **HOME?**

COMING UP, AN OFFER YOU WON'T BELIEVE AT FIRST...

SO TAPE IT AND PLAY IT OVER AND OVER AGAIN —AT **NO** ADDITIONAL COST!

LATE-NIGHT VIEWERS! RUN, DON'T WALK, TO YOUR PHONE **RIGHT NOW** TO TAKE ADVANTAGE OF THIS ONCE-IN-A-CENTURY VIDEO OFFER!

YES, FOR ONLY $29.95, YOU CAN NOW HEAR THE FULL STORY OF THE SIMPSON-GOLDMAN MURDERS AS TOLD BY PRIVATE INVESTIGATOR **O.J. SIMPSON!**

... INCLUDING SHOCKING REVELATIONS LIKE THIS...
MY INVESTIGATION HAS TURNED UP NO EVIDENCE THAT I DID IT.

...AND THIS...
SOMEONE ELSE DID IT— SOMEONE OTHER THAN ME, O.J.

...AND THIS!
PROBABLY THE SAME PERSON WHO PLANTED EVIDENCE ON MY HANDS, MY SOCKS, MY GLOVES, MY BRONCO...
WATCH AGAIN AND AGAIN! GREAT FOR PARTIES! ACT **NOW!**
... MY CARPET, MY BEDROOM, MY DRIVEWAY, MY LAWN...
©B Trudeau

I'M A HUGE FAN OF YOUR EARLY WORK, MR. DOONESBURY.
WHY, THANK YOU.

YOU'VE HELD UP NICELY! YOU KNOW, CONSIDERING...
YEAH.

The Doonesbury Anthology
PART 12

WELL, THE WHOLE COMMUNE THING STARTED OUT AS A LARK. WE WERE JUST SEVEN MIDDLE CLASS KIDS IN OFF-CAMPUS HOUSING...

IN THE EARLY DAYS, WE WEREN'T DRAWN VERY WELL, SO WE DIDN'T HAVE MUCH OF AN AUDIENCE. BUT WE HAD THIS ENERGY, YOU KNOW? WE WERE A TIGHT LITTLE BAND.

SOME OF WHAT WENT ON WAS AMAZING. LIKE THE TIME ZONKER AND THE WHOLE FOOTBALL SQUAD SHOWED UP STONED AND NAKED FOR A GAME...

AARGGH!
ANYONE SEEN THE BALL? WHAT? DID I SAY SOMETHING?
MAYBE. LET ME THINK...
10

OF COURSE, THAT ONE NEVER MADE IT INTO PRINT. TOO OUTRAGEOUS FOR ITS DAY.
THIS WAS BEFORE THE CULTURE HAD BEEN TRASHED.
GB Trudeau

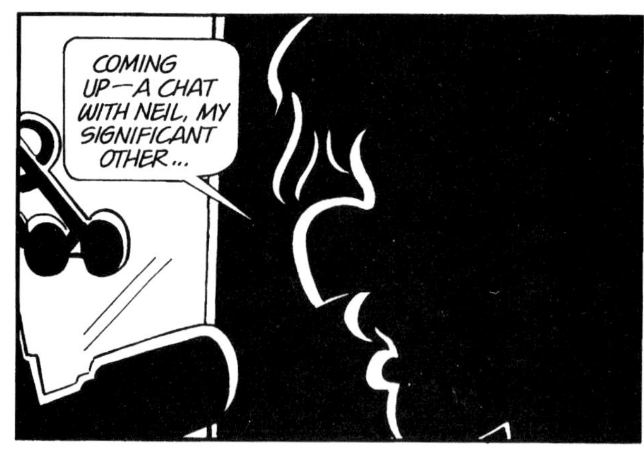
COMING UP—A CHAT WITH NEIL, MY SIGNIFICANT OTHER...

HE'LL BE TELLING US WHY MEETING ME WAS THE BEST THING THAT EVER HAPPENED TO HIM!

IF YOU'RE JUST JOINING US, I'M STILL TALKING TO **NEIL**—ARTIST, DOCTOR, LECTURER, AND, MOST IMPORTANT, MY NEW **ROOMMATE**!

NEIL, THEY SAID WE WOULDN'T LAST, DIDN'T THEY?
WELL, MARK, ANYONE WHO SAID THAT NEVER TALKED TO ME!

NOR ME, NEIL! OKAY, LET'S OPEN UP THE LINES, SHALL WE? IS THE CALLER THERE?

YEAH, MARK, I JUST WANTED TO SAY I THINK IT'S GREAT THAT YOU AND NEIL ARE STILL TOGETHER...

EVERYONE'S ENTITLED TO BE HAPPY, MAN, BUT I DO HAVE ONE QUESTION FOR YOU...
ASK AWAY, MY FRIEND!

AREN'T YOU A LITTLE OLD FOR IMAGINARY PLAYMATES?
UM...
I'LL HANDLE THAT ONE, MARK. WHAT'S YOUR POINT, CALLER?

TIME TO PLAN MY T.V. WEEK...

MAYBE I'LL START OUT WITH A GOOD INFOMERCIAL...

PHIL, BEFORE WE GET STARTED, MAY I SHARE SOMETHING WITH YOUR AUDIENCE?
BY ALL MEANS.

I JUST WANTED TO CONGRAT-ULATE YOU ON YOUR 29 YEARS OF BROADCAST SUCCESS...

YOUR SHOW HAS BEEN A TOUCHSTONE IN MY LIFE. I'VE ALWAYS FOUND IT PROVOCA-TIVE, INFORMATIVE, AND ENTERTAIN-ING...

"DONAHUE" IS WITHOUT QUESTION THE CLASS ACT OF DAYTIME T.V., A PLACE WHERE GUESTS ARE AL-LOWED TO HOLD ON TO THEIR DIG-NITY. YOU'LL BE SORELY MISSED.

UM... THANKS.
YOU'RE WEL-COME!

DOES THIS MEAN YOU'RE NOT GOING TO TAKE OFF YOUR CLOTHES?
NO, NO, I WOULDN'T WANT TO DISAPPOINT THE LADIES!
YEAA!
CLAP! CLAP! CLAP!
GB Trudeau

WISH I KNEW WHAT **REALLY** HAPPENED WITH WHITEWATER...

HUSBANDS AND WIVES NEVER TALK ANYMORE!

OKAY, WHAT'S NEXT?
WHITEWATER, SIR. IT'S STILL KILLING US.

OF COURSE IT IS. BUT WHAT ARE WE SUPPOSED TO DO ABOUT IT?
WELL, SIR, SINCE YOUR WIFE SEEMS TO BE THE ONE WHO'S DRAWING MOST OF THE FIRE...

...PERHAPS SHE SHOULD CONSIDER RESIGNING — AT LEAST FOR A WHILE.

RESIGN AS FIRST LADY?
YES, SIR.

UM...HOW WOULD THAT WORK, EXACTLY?
WELL, SIR...

WOULD I BE HANDLING THE INTERVIEWS FOR HER REPLACEMENT?
NOT EVEN IN YOUR DREAMS, SIR.

To: Rep. Newt Gingrich

☑ Yes! I would like to bid on some of the choice national assets now being liquidated by Congress.

LOT #147 - ALASKAN OLD-GROWTH FORESTS
Opportunity to clear-cut 500-year-old trees. Valued at $50,000 a tree; suggested bid: $1.60 a tree. **MY BID:**________

LOT #183 - WILDERNESS MINERAL RIGHTS
Opportunity to mine pristine wilderness area. Valued at $1 billion+; suggested bid $1,200. **MY BID:**________

LOT #275 - PRIME WESTERN GRAZING LAND
Opportunity to denude taxpayer-maintained range land. Market value: $10.30 per cow and calf per month. Suggested bid: $1.61. **MY BID:**________

Name ________ Street ________

City ________ State ________ Zip ________ Signature ________

SEND TO: The Speaker of the House
U.S. Congress
Washington, D.C. 20515

OR CALL: (202) 225-3121
OR FAX: (202) 225-7733

GOOD LORD...

IT'S MIDNIGHT, AND EVERY LIGHT IN THE BUILDING IS STILL ON!

MAY I HAVE YOUR ATTENTION, PLEASE?

LATELY I'VE BEEN NOTICING THAT MORE AND MORE OF YOU HAVE BEEN SPENDING THE NIGHT HERE CRASHING DEADLINES.

NO PRODUCT LAUNCH IS WORTH THAT KIND OF SACRIFICE. HIGHLY STRESSED, CHRONICALLY FATIGUED EMPLOYEES CAN'T GIVE THEIR BEST, AND I NEED YOUR BEST!

FROM NOW ON, I'M HAVING THE POWER SHUT OFF IN THE BUILDING AT 5:00 P.M.! I WANT YOU TO GO HOME, LEAD LIVES, REST. WE CAN'T BUILD A FUTURE BY TRASHING THE PRESENT.

HE'S GONE MAD.
THE COMPANY'LL **CRASH**! WE'LL BE THE NEXT **APPLE**!
WE BETTER TAKE THIS TO THE BOARD.
GB Trudeau

SIGH...
T

Enjoy cola
YOU'RE IN A **MAJOR** GUILT SPIRAL, GIRL...

YOU'RE LOOKIN' BUMMED TODAY, MAN...
THAT'S BECAUSE I AM.

I JUST DON'T KNOW WHAT TO DO ABOUT ALEX...

WHEN I GO SEE HER, IT'S NOTHING BUT ACRIMONY. MIKE SAYS SHE'S ANGRY FOR **DAYS** AFTERWARD.

BUT IF I **CAN'T** SEE HER, I'LL GO CRAZY! SHE'S MY DAUGHTER, AND I MISS HER INCREDIBLY!

MAYBE YOU COULD JUST STALK HER, MAN.
ZEKE, WHY AM I STILL WITH YOU?

THINK THEY'LL CLIP THIS PART?
NAH...

PEOPLE HAVE LIMITED DOOR/ BULLETIN BOARD SPACE.

MIKE... MIKE, LOOK!
OH... HI, THERE!

THANKS FOR PAUSING TO READ THIS!
YEAH, THANKS...

YOU'RE PROBABLY WONDERING WHY SOMEONE TOOK THE TROUBLE TO CLIP THIS STRIP AND POST IT ON HIS/HER DOOR/BULLETIN BOARD!

WELL, THE ANSWER'S VERY SIMPLE! THE PERSON TO WHOSE BULLETIN BOARD/DOOR THIS STRIP IS AFFIXED THOUGHT YOU'D APPRECIATE A CHUCKLE DURING YOUR BUSY DAY!

PRETTY CONSIDERATE, HUH?
THIS PERSON MUST BE A PEACH!
©B Trudeau

YOU SHOULD GIVE HIM/HER SOME MONEY!
THAT'S RIGHT! JUST LEAVE IT ON HIS/HER DESK!

SO WHERE DO YOU WANT TO GO, KIM?
HOW ABOUT CAFÉ CAMEO?

CAFÉ CAMEO?
IT'S A NEW THEME CLUB DEVOTED TO THE NEAR-FAMOUS...

OLD SITCOM STARS, ONE-HIT ROCKERS, ANYONE WHO WAS ALMOST SOMEONE! SOME NIGHTS THE PLACE IS **SWARMING** WITH PEOPLE WHO LOOK VAGUELY FAMILIAR!

WHAT A DRAW.
YOU NEVER KNOW, MIKE - YOU MIGHT SPOT STEVE FORBES.
GB Trudeau

HI, FOLKS — WELCOME TO **CAFÉ CAMEO**, HOME OF THE NEAR-GREATS! MY NAME'S CHUCK, AND I'M WORKING THE DOOR TONIGHT.

LISTEN, WOULD YOU GUYS MIND WAITING HERE IN LINE FOR AWHILE? WE'RE TRYING TO MAKE THE CLUB LOOK HOT.
SURE, CHUCK!

Café Cameo
GB Trudeau

OKAY, YOU CAN GO IN. THANKS.
NO PROB-LEM.
HEY, **LOOK!** IT'S WHATS-HIS-FACE!
Café Cameo

Also Starring
CAFÉ CAMEO. GOTTA LOVE THE THEME.
I KNOW. IT'S **SO** DOPE...
Café Cameo

THE BUZZ ON THIS PLACE IS THAT **TWO** OF THE ORIGINAL BRADY BUNCH HANG HERE! AND THE SHIRTLESS GUY IN THE COKE COMMERCIAL...

IF I SAW... **HEY!** OVER THERE, MIKE — LOOK! IT'S WHAT'S-HER-NAME! THE GIRL WHO USED TO PLAY ALL THOSE BIMBOS!

BOOPSIE!
OH... RIGHT, RIGHT! VERY **GOOD**, MIKE!
GB Trudeau
Café Cameo

MIKE! MY GOSH – WHAT ARE YOU DOING HERE?
I WAS GOING TO ASK YOU THE SAME THING, BOOPSIE!

YOU MEAN YOU DIDN'T HEAR? I'M A BACKER OF CAFÉ CAMEO! ME AND CHARO AND KATO KAELIN AND HEIDI FLEISS AND A GILLIGAN STAR.

AND IT'S GOING GREAT! WE'VE ALREADY GOT CLUBS IN FOUR CITIES!
AMAZING! ARE YOU IN TOWN A LOT?

NO, NO, I JUST FLEW UP HERE FOR JOEY BUTTAFUOCO NIGHT.
JOEY'S HERE? IN SEATTLE?

ANYWAY, I'M FLYING FROM CLUB TO CLUB TO HELP PROMOTE SPECIAL EVENTS!

IT'S SO GREAT MEETING PEOPLE WHO SORT OF RECOGNIZE ME! ALSO, IT ALLOWS ME TO KEEP AN EYE ON MY INVESTMENT...

EXCUSE ME A MOMENT, GUYS. I HAVE TO CALL THE CHEF...

JEAN-CLAUDE? THE CHEESEBURGERS NEED MORE SEAWEED!
SEAWEED?
YOW! WHAT ATTENTION TO DETAIL!

THIS IS LIKE SO GREAT THAT YOU GUYS KNOW EACH OTHER! WHERE DID YOU MEET?
COLLEGE...

WE WENT TO WALDEN TOGETHER. BOOPSIE AND I WERE TWO OF THE FOUNDING MEMBERS OF A COMMUNE.

A COMMUNE? YOU GUYS DID THE COMMUNE THING? WAS IT A MAJOR BOINKFEST?
UH... WELL, NO, NOT REALLY. RIGHT, BOOPSIE?
RIGHT.

YOU DON'T SOUND VERY SURE.
IT WAS A LONG TIME AGO, KIM.
WE'RE MUCH OLDER THAN YOU.

I'M SORRY YOUR YOUNG MAN COULDN'T JOIN US, DEAR...
WELL, THE PAPER MOVED HIM TO THE BUCHANAN CAMPAIGN...

IT'S NOT LIKE COVERING LUGAR. HE HAS TO SPEND A LOT OF TIME TRACKING DOWN REPORTS ON BUCHANAN'S CAMPAIGN STAFF...

IT SEEMS THAT AN UNCOMMONLY HIGH PERCENTAGE OF THEM SUFFER FROM, SHALL WE SAY, BACKGROUND PROBLEMS.

MR. WOLFE? I'M RICK REDFERN...
HEIL. I MEAN, HI.

MR. WOLFE, I WONDER IF I COULD TALK TO YOU ABOUT THE UNUSUALLY HIGH NUMBER OF RACIST STAFFERS THE BUCHANAN CAMPAIGN **SEEMS** TO HAVE ATTRACTED...

NO, BECAUSE YOUR PREMISE IS LUDICROUS! WE DON'T **HAVE** ANY RACIST STAFFERS! THEY'RE ALL ON LEAVE, CLEARING THEIR NAMES!

WHY? BECAUSE PAT BUCHANAN DOESN'T HAVE A BIGOTED BONE IN HIS BODY! HE **DESPISES** INTOLERANCE IN ANY GUISE, AND WILL **NOT** TOLERATE IT IN HIS CAMPAIGN!

WYATT? YOU BUSY?
LATER, EARL, **LATER!**

EXCUSE ME, BUT WAS THAT STAFFER WEARING A HOOD?
WHAT, HE'S NOT ENTITLED TO PRIVACY? IS THAT WHAT YOU'RE SAYING, MR. REDBURG?

LET ME TELL YOU WHAT THAT HOOD'S ABOUT, OKAY? IT'S ABOUT THINGS GETTING SO BAD IN THIS COUNTRY THAT A WHITE ANGLO MALE IS AFRAID TO SHOW HIS **FACE!**

AND **THAT'S** WHY WE NEED PAT! WHO **ELSE** REACHES OUT TO THE VICTIMS OF AFFIRMATIVE ACTION? WHERE **ELSE** IS THE YOUNG, CONCERNED SKINHEAD SUPPOSED TO GO?

I GUESS I NEVER THOUGHT ABOUT IT BEFORE...
WHY AM I NOT SURPRISED, ABE? IT'S ABE, ISN'T IT?

YOU SEE, MR. REDSTEIN, WHAT YOU PEOPLE IN THE LIBERAL MEDIA HAVE MISSED IS THE **INCLUSIVENESS** OF THIS CAMPAIGN...

PAT BUCHANAN IS THE **ONLY** MAJOR CANDIDATE TO REACH OUT TO THE FORGOTTEN SKINHEAD, TO THE FORGOTTEN BIGOT, TO THE FORGOTTEN JEW-BAITER!

PAT **CONNECTS** WITH THESE FOLKS, HE KNOWS HOW THEY THINK, HE SPEAKS THEIR LANGUAGE!

WHAT LANGUAGE IS THAT?
CODE. HE'S FLUENT.

MR. WOLFE, IT'S BEEN SAID THAT BUCHANAN COULDN'T HAVE BEATEN GRAMM IN LOUISIANA WITHOUT THE HELP OF DAVID DUKE...
NONSENSE!

PAT WENT TO ELABORATE LENGTHS **NOT** TO GET PHOTOGRAPHED WITH DUKE. HE KNOWS THAT DAVID PUSHES A LOT OF BUTTONS WITH THE NEW YORK MEDIA CABAL.

BUT PAT BUCHANAN LIVES IN THE REAL WORLD! AND THE FACT IS, YOU **CANNOT** WIN A G.O.P. PRIMARY IN LOUISIANA WITHOUT THE SUPPORT OF THE NAZIS!

I... I DIDN'T KNOW THAT.
NEITHER DID GRAMM. HE MIGHT AS WELL HAVE CAMPAIGNED IN BELGIUM.

ONE LAST POINT, MR. ROTHFIELD: YOU MEDIA CABALISTS CAN RAIL ALL YOU WANT, BUT THE BUCHANAN MOVEMENT **CANNOT** BE DENIED!

PAT'S REACHING OUT TO PEOPLE WHO HAVE NEVER BEEN REACHED OUT TO BEFORE. HE'S EMPOWERING THE FORMERLY POWERLESS, AND THEY **LOVE** HIM FOR IT!

DO YOU KNOW WHAT YOU GET WHEN YOU BRING TOGETHER EVERY PROTECTIONIST, ISOLATIONIST, ULTRANATIONALIST, SEGREGATIONIST, ANTI-IMMIGRATIONIST, WHITE SUPREMACIST IN THE COUNTRY?

A DEMOCRATIC CONGRESS?
PROBABLY.
BUT MAYBE-JUST MAYBE-AN EIGHT-YEAR REICH!

HEY, YOU. WHATCHA DOING?
DIGITAL CAMPAIGNING...

I JUST SENT STEVE FORBES' PROGRAM TO OUR ENTIRE CUSTOMER BASE. I REALIZE I'M KIND OF ABUSING THE COMPANY SYSTEM, BUT WHAT THE HELL...

SOME PEOPLE STEAL PAPERCLIPS. I SEND OUT 200,000 E-MAILS!
I DON'T LIKE IT. YOU USED DISCRETIONARY TIME THINKING ABOUT STEVE FORBES INSTEAD OF ME?

YOU'RE RIGHT— HOW DO I STOP IT?
TOO LATE. I CAN'T WAIT TO SEE HOW YOU'LL MAKE IT UP TO ME!

I KNOW YOU DON'T QUITE GET THE STEVE FORBES THING, KIM, BUT TRUST ME—HE'S ONE OF US. HE'S A CORE LIBERTARIAN GEEK!

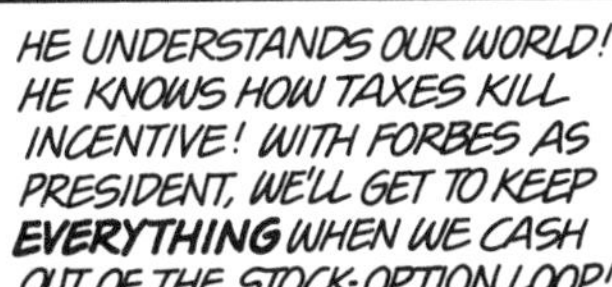
HE UNDERSTANDS OUR WORLD! HE KNOWS HOW TAXES KILL INCENTIVE! WITH FORBES AS PRESIDENT, WE'LL GET TO KEEP EVERYTHING WHEN WE CASH OUT OF THE STOCK-OPTION LOOP!

LISTEN TO ME.
YOU SAY YOU USED TO LIVE IN A COMMUNE?

SO WHAT ARE YOU DOING HERE ANYWAY, KIM? I THOUGHT YOU WERE IN A SERIOUS CRUNCH MODE TODAY.
WELL, I AM...

BUT I WAS SITTING THERE HUNCHED OVER MY MAC, TOTALLY GEEKED OUT ON A KILLER RUN OF CODE, WHEN SUDDENLY I FELT A MAJOR NEED FOR FACE-TIME WITH MY PERSON!

I'M YOUR PERSON?
IF THAT'S COOL WITH YOU.

UM...SURE! DOES THIS MEAN DATES?
NO, SLEEPOVERS. MIKE, THE DATING THING IS VERY 20 YEARS AGO!

LOOK, KIM, BEFORE WE GO ANY FURTHER, I GOTTA ASK YOU— YOU'RE NOT UNCOMFORTABLE WITH OUR AGE DIFFERENCE?
NOT AT ALL. WHY WOULD I BE?

MIKE, I GREW UP IN A WORLD DOMINATED BY BOOMERS. YOUR CULTURE WAS INESCAPABLE. AND LETTERMAN GAVE MY AGE GROUP THE TOOLS TO ASSIMILATE.

IT'S TRUE I DIDN'T EXPERIENCE THE NUCLEAR FAMILY, DISCO AND '60S T.V. FIRST-HAND, BUT BY THE TIME I WAS 15, I COULD REFER TO ALL OF THEM IN A HIP, KNOWING WAY.
GB Trudeau

AMAZING... I DIDN'T GO IRONIC UNTIL I WAS 30!
QUIZ ME ON "GILLIGAN'S ISLAND." GO AHEAD, ASK ME ANYTHING!

SEE, MIKE, EVEN WITH THE AGE DISPARITY, WE'RE NOT THAT DIFFERENT. SURE, YOU CAME BY YOUR CYNICISM THROUGH YEARS OF DISILLUSIONMENT, WHEREAS I SIMPLY GREW UP CYNICAL...

BUT ON PLANET DOWNSIZE, RANDOM DESPAIR BECOMES THE DEFAULT PARADIGM FOR ALL WORKER BEES! IT'S WHERE THE GENERATIONS—YOUR TRIBE AND MINE—NOW CONVERGE!

GB Trudeau

WANT ME TO SCROLL THAT BY YOU AGAIN?
PLEASE. AND COULD I HAVE A HARD COPY?

YOU KNOW, KIM, I'M NOT SO SURE THE SLEEPOVER PART OF OUR RELATIONSHIP IS GOING TO WORK OUT...
WHAT? WHY NOT?

WELL, YOU LIVE IN A GROUP HOUSE WITH FIVE OTHER TECHIES. AND I LIVE IN A CONDO WITH A SEVEN-YEAR-OLD. NEITHER PLACE IS VERY CONDUCIVE TO A COURTSHIP.

"COURTSHIP"? DID YOU REALLY JUST SAY "COURTSHIP," MIKE?

I DID, BUT TO MY CREDIT, I INSTANTLY REGRETTED IT.
YOU'RE SECOND-GENERATION GEEK, AREN'T YOU?

ALEX, I'D LIKE YOU TO MEET DADDY'S NEW FRIEND, KIM ROSENTHAL...
HI, ALEX!

LISTEN, I HAVE TO MAKE A FEW CALLS, SO WHY DON'T YOU GUYS JUST HANG FOR AWHILE, OKAY?

I ALREADY HAVE A MOTHER.
SO DO I. WANT TO PLAY THE NEW NBA ALL-STARS?

YOU'VE GOT THE NEW NBA ALL-STARS DISK?
EVEN BETTER-I'VE GOT THE 1997 BETA VERSION!

GET OUT! WHO GAVE IT TO YOU?
WE'RE PUBLISHING IT. I'M DOING THE BUG-CHECKING.

YOU'RE A BUG-CHECKER? THAT'S YOUR JOB?
SOMETIMES. WHY?

WHY? BUG-CHECKING IS BRUTALLY COOL!
AH, ANOTHER CRAZY KID WITH A DREAM.

SO CHECK THIS OUT, OKAY? IF YOU CLICK ON DENNIS RODMAN'S SNEAKERS, HIS HAIR CHANGES COLOR!

THAT'S SO AWESOME!
IT'S WHAT WE CALL EASTER EGG FUNCTIONALITY—A LITTLE SURPRISE FOR THOSE IN THE KNOW...

YOU KNOW, KIM, I'M SO GLAD IT'S YOU WHO'S DADDY'S FRIEND! WHEN HE TOLD ME HE WAS SEEING SOMEONE AT WORK, I WAS AFRAID THAT... THAT...
THAT WHAT, ALEX?

I WAS AFRAID SHE MIGHT BE FROM MARKETING.
YOU POOR KID! WHY DIDN'T YOU JUST ASK?

KIM, ARE YOU AMERICAN? YOU DON'T LOOK AMERICAN.

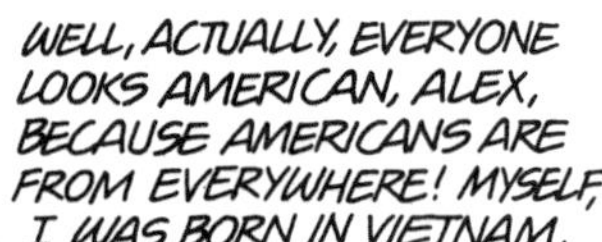
WELL, ACTUALLY, EVERYONE LOOKS AMERICAN, ALEX, BECAUSE AMERICANS ARE FROM EVERYWHERE! MYSELF, I WAS BORN IN VIETNAM.

VIETNAM... OH, SURE, RIGHT.

THAT'S IN MICHIGAN, ISN'T IT?
HMM... NOT SURE. LET'S CHECK IN ENCARTA, OKAY?

HEY, KIM, YOU WANT TO SEE MY HOME-GIRL PAGE?
YOU'RE ON THE WEB? NOT EVEN!

EVEN! SEE! IT'S MOSTLY FOR JUNIOR GEEKS—GAME REVIEWS AND STUFF...
ALEX, I'M IMPRESSED! DID YOU DESIGN IT ALL YOURSELF?

UH-HUH. GRANDMA GAVE ME THE SITE FOR CHRISTMAS, BUT I THINK SHE'S GOING TO SHUT IT DOWN SOON...
WHAT? BUT IT'S BEAUTIFUL! HOW **COULD** SHE?

WELL, SHE'S ALREADY DROPPED $27,000 ON IT...
YOW.
YOU KNOW, I **HEARD** THE WEB WAS IN TROUBLE...

...AND THEN AFTER THAT WE JUST GEEKED OUT ON THE BETA GAMES I BROUGHT.

OH, AND I GAVE HER SOME SKITTLES, WHICH WAS COOL, BECAUSE IT TURNS OUT THAT'S **HER** FAVORITE FOOD, TOO...

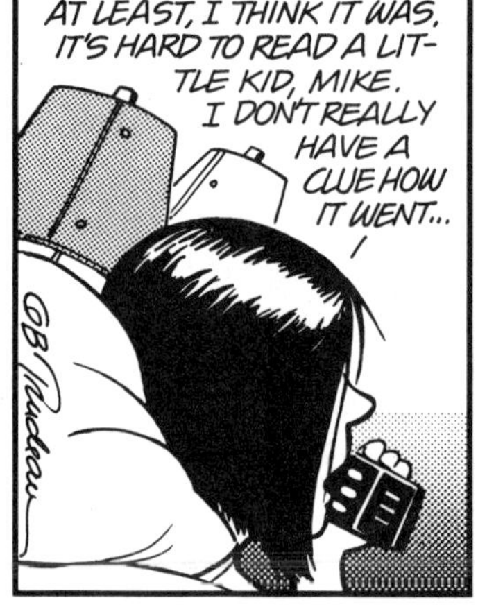
AT LEAST, I THINK IT WAS. IT'S HARD TO READ A LITTLE KID, MIKE. I DON'T REALLY HAVE A CLUE HOW IT WENT...

DAD, CAN I WEAR MY HAIR IN MY FACE?
TRUST ME, IT WENT FINE.